To Amber

With love from

Isabela,

Tim

and

Megan

2020!

THE BLOCKBUSTER BIBLE

BEHIND THE

SCENES OF THE

BIBLE STORY

Text copyright © 2019 Andrew Prichard
This edition copyright © 2019 Lion Hudson IP Limited

The right of Andrew Prichard to be identified as the author of this work has been asserted by him in accordance with the Copyright, Designs and Patents Act 1988.

Published by
Lion Hudson Limited
Wilkinson House, Jordan Hill Business Park
Banbury Road, Oxford OX2 8DR, England
www.lionhudson.com

ISBN 978 0 7459 7779 9

First edition 2019

Acknowledgements
Design and illustrations by Collaborate
A catalogue record for this book is available from the British Library

Printed and bound in China, May 2019, LH54

THE BLOCKBUSTER BIBLE

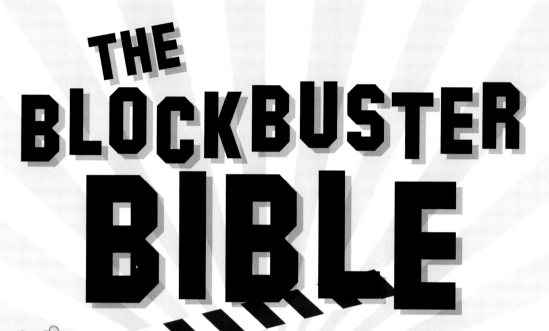

BEHIND THE

SCENES OF THE

BIBLE STORY

Andrew Prichard

SCENE SELECTION

SPECIAL FEATURES

THE OLD TESTAMENT

ACT 1: IN THE BEGINNING

ACT 2: SPOILED BY SIN

ACT 3: COVENANTS

ACT 4: NATION ISRAEL

ACT 5: PROPHETS AND KINGS

INTERMISSION

THE NEW TESTAMENT
ACT 6: THE PROMISED KING

ACT 7: GLOBAL GOSPEL

ACT 8: NEW CREATION

SPECIAL FEATURES:

THE MAKING OF THE BIBLE

Welcome to God's library!

Hi, I'm Freddie! But my friends call me 3D Freddie. Probably because I never take off these cool specs. I love making history three-dimensional! Here's the guided tour – how the Bible was made!

Welcome to God's library. It's all his! He says he "breathed" it all. He inspired the writers to write. People often call the Bible God's Word. "Bible" isn't a made-up word. It's Greek. It means "books".

The Bible is actually a library of many different books. 66 books, in fact! Split into two parts: The Old Testament and the New Testament. "Testament" means "agreement", or "way of doing things". It's God's way of doing things.

Did you know? More than 40 different people wrote it! In fact, it took them 1,600 years!

They wrote it from about 1500 BC to about AD 100. That's what I call epic!

GENESIS
EXODUS
LEVITICUS
NUMBERS
DEUTERONOMY

JOSHUA
JUDGES
RUTH
1 SAMUEL
2 SAMUEL

1 KINGS
2 KINGS
1 CHRONICLES
2 CHRONICLES
EZRA

NEHEMIAH
ESTHER
JOB
PSALMS
PROVERBS

ECCLESIASTES
SONG OF SONGS
ISAIAH
JEREMIAH
LAMENTATIONS
EZEKIEL
DANIEL

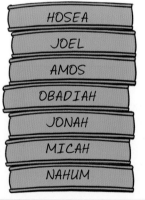

HOSEA
JOEL
AMOS
OBADIAH
JONAH
MICAH
NAHUM

HABAKKUK
ZEPHANIAH
HAGGAI
ZECHARIAH
MALACHI

The Old Testament

ASK 3D FREDDIE

How popular is the Bible?

Hugely! It's the bestselling book of all time, with over 6 billion Bibles in the world today! But many countries make it illegal to have one. So it's not always popular.

BIBLE WRITING STYLES

The Bible isn't all the same. That might get boring! It takes over 70 hours to read the whole thing out loud. Good thing there are different writing styles!

Everyone writes in a different way, and people write for different reasons: entertainment, history, poetry, record-keeping, letter writing. I could go on.

Here are five writing styles in the Bible…

Law
These books talk about God's agreement with Israel. Moses is believed to have written these books and Jewish people call them the Torah.

History
The true story about how Israel became a nation, how they rebelled against God, and what he did about it. True stories about Jesus are called Gospels.

Poetry
Some writers wrote songs and proverbs. They are full of wise sayings about the meaning of life. They're nice to dip into any time you like.

Prophecy
Prophets wrote God's message to his people.God has a lot to say! They often talk about the future, both good and bad. Listen sharp!

Letters
Jesus' friends wrote to each other, telling them what Jesus has done and how they should live. Some letters are tiny. Some are massive! All are juicy.

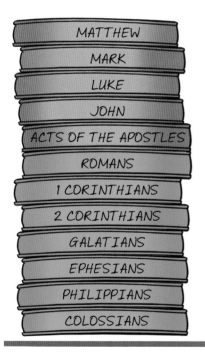

MATTHEW
MARK
LUKE
JOHN
ACTS OF THE APOSTLES
ROMANS
1 CORINTHIANS
2 CORINTHIANS
GALATIANS
EPHESIANS
PHILIPPIANS
COLOSSIANS

1 THESSALONIANS
2 THESSALONIANS
1 TIMOTHY
2 TIMOTHY
TITUS
PHILEMON
HEBREWS
JAMES
1 PETER
2 PETER
1 JOHN
2 JOHN

The New Testament

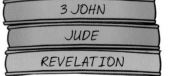

3 JOHN
JUDE
REVELATION

KEY

 =Law

 =History

=Poetry   =Prophecy   =Letters

SPECIAL FEATURES:

THE BIG STORY OF THE BIBLE

The Bible story

Hello too! I'm Popcorn Sally. I love a good story – and what's better than a true story? The Bible story is about God. It's His story. History! Here are three storylines for the Bible. Look out for them as you read this book.

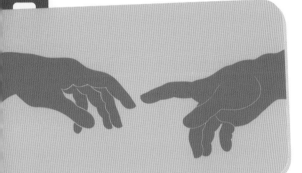

THEME 1 Living With God

God and his people live together, the truest of friends. But trouble looms. Adam and Eve turn away and old friends are separated. But God never gives up on them. He joins his people in the Temple, and sends his Son Jesus to live with them, before beginning an eternity with them in paradise. Reviews call LIVING WITH GOD an uplifting masterpiece, as God leads a very surprising cast to live together forever.

THEME 2 God's Promises

Abraham and David are forgotten men until God makes them promises they will never forget. Childless Abraham will have as many children as the stars and the sand, and King David will have a descendant to rule forever. Who will they be? Watch and find out. GOD'S PROMISES is an unforgettable story of love, commitment, and faithfulness, and will top the box office for countless generations.

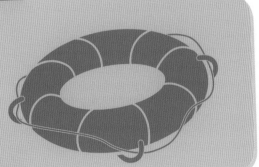

THEME 3 God's Rescue

Humankind faces a terrible problem. The problem of the human heart. Unable to change, they need a rescuer. A Chosen One. Facing incredible odds, the rescuer must live a perfect life and die a perfect death to save his people from being cut off from their Creator forever. GOD'S RESCUE is an award-winning film about waiting for Jesus, the Chosen One, and his heroic victory over sin and death. A must-see.

SELECTED HIGHLIGHTS (AND LOWLIGHTS!)

There are some super-famous parts of the Bible story. See if you recognize any of these and feel free to flick ahead to them using the page numbers.

Adam and Eve eat the Fruit (page 16) The first humans listen to the snake and disobey God.

Abraham about to Sacrifice Isaac (page 29) God tests old Abraham to see if he loves him more than his only son. (Isaac survives!)

David and Goliath (page 64) Young shepherd David defeats hulk Goliath with a slingshot!

Daniel and the Lions' Den (page 83) Faithful Daniel is thrown to the lions for obeying God.

Jesus' Birth (page 100) The chosen saviour is born and lies in a manger.

Feeding of the 5,000 (page 113) Jesus feeds 5,000 with two fish and five loaves.

Jesus' Crucifixion (page 132) Jesus dies among criminals and suffers for the sins of the world.

Saul Becomes a Christian (page 146) Jesus meets Saul on his way to arrest Jesus' followers.

ASK POPCORN SALLY

Can you tell each Bible storyline in seven words?

Maybe?! How are these? God turns people from enemies into friends. God keeps promises when it looks impossible. Jesus dies to forgive his sinful friends.

Timeline: The Bible Story

It's a long story, but here it is in a nutshell. The story leads up to Jesus and then looks back on him. Really, it's all about him. He completes all the storylines.

BC
(Before Christ. Dates are approximate.)

In the beginning, God makes the world and gives humans the special position as his vice-kings and queens.

Adam and Eve rebel against God, instead listening to the devil.

Adam and Eve's children spiral out of control, killing, dying, choosing evil, and rebelling against God.

God makes three great promises to Abraham: land, nation, blessing.

Isaac fathers Jacob who fathers Joseph; the family (Israel) moves to Egypt.

SOON AFTER...   **2000 BC**   **2000 – 1800**

Israelites arrive at the Promised Land; refuse to trust God and enter.

Israelites leave Egypt in the Exodus.

Moses is born; adopted as a prince of Egypt.

New Pharaoh makes Israelites into slaves.

Israelites wander in the desert for 40 years.

1450 – 1410   **1450**   **1450**   **1500**   **1800**

Joshua leads Israelites into Canaan and Israel becomes a nation.

Judges lead Israel for short periods; Israel worships other gods.

Saul rules Israel as king; puts himself first.

David rules Israel; "the man after God's heart" (loves God).

Solomon rules Israel; builds the Temple and worships other gods.

1410   **1375 – 1050**   **1050 – 1010**   **1010 – 971**   **971 – 931**

Exiles trickle back to Jerusalem; rebuild Temple and city walls.

Babylon destroys Jerusalem; takes more exiles.

Babylon attacks Jerusalem (capital of Judah); takes away exiles.

Assyria destroys Israel; foreign people live in its land.

Kingdom divides in two: Israel (north) and Judah (south).

538 – 445   **586**   **597**   **722**   **931**

Jesus is born in Bethlehem.

Jesus dies on a cross and rises again.

The Holy Spirit comes at Pentecost.

Saul becomes a Christian on the way to Damascus.

Jesus' followers write letters across the Mediterranean.

5   **28 – 30 AD**   **33 (OR 30)**   **33 (OR 34)**   **40 – 95**

Jesus begins work as a teacher.

Paul (Saul) martyred in Rome under Emperor Nero.

Jesus' followers write four Gospels: Matthew, Mark, Luke, and John.

64 – 67   **53 – 90**

AD
(Anno Domini. Latin for "from the year of the Lord.")

THE OLD TESTAMENT

TICKET: ADMIT ONE
THE BIBLE STORY
Front Row Seat
Curtains up at... NOW!

ACT 1: IN THE BEGINNING

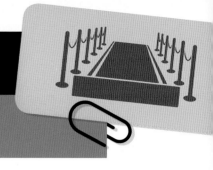

SCENE 1: VIP HUMANKIND

Lights, camera, action!

Nothing exists. Then God calls for a beginning (Genesis).
"Light! Space! Land!" In days 1–3 he makes the world, and in 4–6 he fills it. He saves the best until last.

DESIGN: THE SEVEN DAYS OF CREATION

Day 1

"Let there be light! I will call the light day and the darkness night… It's good!"

Day 2

"Let there be a space between the sea below and above. I call it sky… It's good!"

Day 3

"Let there be land and seas. Let there be many fruit-bearing plants… It's good!"

Day 4

"Let there be lights, for the day and the night. Also let there be stars… It's good!"

Day 5

"Let there be many creatures for the sea and many birds for the sky. I bless them to increase in number. It's good!"

Day 6

"Let there be many creatures for the land: livestock, creatures, and wild animals. It's good!

"And let us make humankind in our image. And let them rule over the fish, over the birds, and all the animals that roam the earth. See, now it's very good!"

Day 7

God rests from work and blesses the seventh day as special.

"Very good"

God's world is good until he makes humans. They make it very good! Humans are VIP – Very Important People – and they are vice-rulers over the rest of God's world.

★ ★ ★ ★ ★

Why does God make humans?

Humans are the best!

Humans are different from the rest of creation. God makes them to be like him and he gives them special jobs to do. They are Very Important People!

VIP

In God's image	God made us in his likeness, male and female.
Blessed	God told us to have children and fill the earth.
Rulers	God told us to rule over the fish, the birds, and every living thing on the earth.
Plant eaters	God gave us food: every plant or fruit with seed in it. The animals eat green plants.
Very good	God now calls the world "very good". Humans make the world complete.

HUMANS

HUM

HUMANS

ASK 3D FREDDIE

How old is the world then?

Some say about 14 billion years. Others say about 6,000 years. It depends what you think about the story of creation. Is it literal, or symbolic? In the end, we can't be totally sure.

"In God's image"

Humans are like God as his vice-rulers. They are like photos of God, the great ruler. But they are also unlike him. The creator is much greater than his creatures.

★ ★ ★ ★ ★

Why are humans very important people?

SCENE 2: LIVING WITH GOD

The LORD God

Let's zoom in on how God makes humans. God and humans live together as true friends in the paradise of the Garden of Eden. True delight.

DESIGN: THE GARDEN OF EDEN

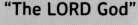

1 The land is bare.

2 The Lord God moulds a man from the ground and breathes the breath of life into him.

3 The Lord God plants a Garden in Eden and puts the man in it.

4 The Lord God makes all kinds of trees grow there. The trees are beautiful and carry good fruit. He also makes the tree of life and the tree of the knowledge of good and evil.

5 One river divides into four rivers: the Pishon, the Gihon, the Tigris, and the Euphrates. The land carries gold, onyx, precious stones, and perfume.

6 The Lord God tells the man to work and care for the Garden of Eden. He says, "You may eat from any tree, except from the tree of the knowledge of good and evil. If you do, you will surely die."

"The LORD God"

God makes humans to know him personally. His personal name is written as LORD in the Bible. He lives close to them and gives them special instructions.

★ ★ ★ ★ ★

Why is the Garden a place of delight?

Finding a helper

God gives the man a job. He is God's vice-ruler – a gardener and guardian over creation. The man needs a helper, and they will fill the world and take care of it together.

HELPER 1 – ANIMALS

The Lord God says, "It is not good for the man to be alone. I will make him a suitable helper." So the Lord brings all kinds of animals and all kinds of birds he had formed to the man to see what he would name them. The man names every animal and every bird, but Adam finds no suitable helper.

HELPER 2 – WOMAN

The Lord God makes the first woman. The man says, "At last, someone like me. I will name her 'woman'."

So a man leaves his parents to join his wife, and they become one. The man and his wife were both naked but not embarrassed.

ASK POPCORN SALLY

Why does God make a tree they cannot eat from?

To see whether Adam and the woman obey God! He made a rule and gave them a choice. Will they obey? If there's no choice, they have no free will! The tree was a good thing!

"Not good"

The world is very good, but it's not perfect yet. It needs to be filled and looked after. Adam (meaning "man") and the woman are perfect partners to do this together.

★ ★ ★ ★ ★

Why is the woman a perfect match for Adam?

ACT 2: SPOILED BY SIN

SCENE 1: THE FALL

Turning against God

Adam and his wife have clear instructions. They rule God's world, but a crafty snake arrives: God's enemy. Will they ignore it, or turn their backs on God, their friend?

Disobeying God

Snake: "Did God really say you cannot eat from any tree in the Garden?"

Eve: "We may eat from any tree, but not from the tree of the knowledge of good and evil. If we eat from it, or even touch it, we will die."

Snake: "That's a lie! You will surely not die. God knows that you will be like God and know good and evil."

Eve sees the good fruit and the chance to be wise. Takes some, eats, gives some to her husband. See they are naked and sew together fig leaves as clothes.

The Lord: "Where are you, Adam?" Adam: "I heard you walking in the Garden and I was afraid of you. I hid because I was naked."

The Lord: "Who told you that you were naked? Have you eaten from the tree of the knowledge of good and evil?"

Adam: "The woman you put here gave me some fruit and I ate."

The Lord: "What have you done?" Eve: "The snake lied to me and I ate."

"The snake lied"

Adam and the woman listen to the snake and ignore God. They rule as if he does not exist. This is called sin and the Bible says all people are like Adam and his wife.

★ ★ ★ ★ ★

How is the world spoiled?

Adam and Eve move away

God is holy and cannot live with his sinful people. He is also fair and cannot ignore their sin. He punishes them and sends them away from him.

God Punishes

The Lord: "Snake, most cursed animal! You will eat the dust and slither on your belly. You and the woman's descendants will hate each other. One of her descendants will crush your head, but you will strike his heel."

The Lord: "You will have great pain when you give birth. You and your husband will disagree, and he will lead you."

The Lord: "Your world will be cursed, and your work will now be hard. You will sweat as you work, and the ground will grow thorns and thistles as you do."

The Lord: "One day you will die and return to the ground; you are dust and to dust you will return."

Adam: "I name you Eve because you are the 'mother of all the living'."

God makes Adam and Eve clothes from animal skins.

God sends Adam and Eve east, away from the Garden.

God places two angels and a flashing sword to guard the way back to the tree of life.

FLASH-FORWARD >>>

… to the Cross (page 132). God promises a snake crusher. Jesus will defeat the devil. He will die as he pays for sins.

"Clothes of skins"

God is still generous, even when Adam and Eve sin. They don't deserve his gifts, but he covers up their embarrassment anyway. He still loves them.

★ ★ ★ ★ ★

How does God punish but also be generous?

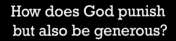

17

SCENE 2: SIN AND DEATH SPREAD

Murder spreads

God gives sons to Adam and Eve. Is one of them the promised snake crusher to defeat the devil? No. Instead, they keep on sinning and their sin gets worse.

Cain Murders Abel

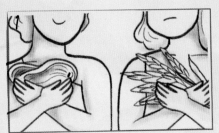

1

Abel the shepherd offers God the best bits of his firstborn lambs. Cain the crop farmer offers some of his crops.

2

God likes Abel's offering but not Cain's.

3

The Lord: "Why are you angry? Do what's right! Sin wants to conquer you, but you must rule over it."

4

Cain murders Abel in a field.

5

The Lord: "Where is Abel, your brother?"
Cain: "I don't know! Must I care for him?"

6

The Lord: "Your brother's blood cries out from the ground! You killed Abel! Now your crops will not grow and you will wander the earth."

7

Cain: "This is too much! I will wander and someone may kill me!"

8

The Lord: "No! If they do, I will punish them seven times more." God marks Cain so no one will kill him.

Cain wanders away to Nod, further east from Eden.

"Rule over it"

Cain fails to rule his sin. He ignores God's warning, murders Abel, and lies to God. He moves even further east from Eden. Their sin is quickly getting worse.

Why does Cain murder Abel?

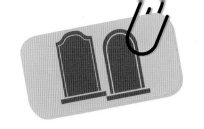

Death spreads

God promised Adam and Eve that they would die if they ate from the tree of the knowledge of good and evil. We get a list of their descendants, who all die.

Adam's Descendants Die

1

Adam fathers a son in his image, Seth. Adam lives 930 years and dies.

2

Seth fathers Enosh. Seth lives 912 years and dies.

Enosh fathers Kenan. Enosh lives 905 years and dies.

3

Kenan fathers Mahalalel. Kenan lives 910 years and dies.

Mahalalel fathers Jared. Mahalalel lives 895 years and dies.

4

Jared fathers Enoch. Jared lives 962 years and dies. Enoch fathers Methuselah.

5

Enoch walks faithfully with God for 300 years.

6

Enoch is no more; God takes him away.

7

Methuselah fathers Lamech. Methuselah lives 969 years and dies.

Lamech fathers Noah. Lamech lives 777 years and dies.

8

Noah fathers Shem, Ham, and Japheth.

"Walks faithfully with God"

God spares Enoch the sadness of death. Enoch lives with God on earth, and then lives with God in heaven. God is still generous.

★ ★ ★ ★ ★

How is Enoch different from Adam?

ASK 3D FREDDIE

Were people going to live forever?

Yes, and the Bible says they still can. Adam and Eve ate from the tree of life, and the book of Revelation shows God's new creation where people will eat from the tree of life again.

Violence spreads

Humans are increasing in number, but they live without obeying God. They keep turning away from him and their sin gets even worse. So God takes action.

God Sends a Flood

1. Men see beautiful women, like them, and take lots of them as wives.

2. The Lord: "Humans will not live forever. No more than 120 years."

3. The people are wicked, violent, and corrupt. Their hearts only choose evil, all the time. God regrets making them.

4. Noah is a friend of God and walks with him.

5. The Lord: "Violence and corruption fill the earth so I will wipe them away with a flood. Noah, make an ark and bring into it a male and female of every living thing."

6. Noah finishes an ark. The Lord: "In seven days it will rain for 40 days."

7. Every living thing with the breath of life dies. God wipes them away.

8. The flood lasts 150 days and begins to dry up.

"Their hearts only choose evil"

God sees his people's hearts. They also "see, like, and take" whatever they want. God will recreate the world with Noah, even though Noah is not perfect either.

★ ★ ★ ★ ★

<<< FLASHBACK

... to the Creation (page 12). God promises rain in seven days. It reminds us of the seven days God spent creating the earth. God wants to start again.

Why does God send a flood?

Rebellion spreads

Even after the flood, sin keeps spreading. Noah's descendants move further east, and away from God. They want to live away from him and they plot rebellion.

The Tower of Babel

The people speak one language and settle together.

Builders: "Let's make bricks and mortar."

Builders: "Let's build ourselves a city and a tower. Its top will reach the skies!"

Builders: "Let's make a name for ourselves, and not spread over the whole earth as God wants."

God comes down and then sees the city and tower. (Not very high yet!)

The Lord: "See, they are one people with one language."

The Lord: "Let's mix up their languages so they don't understand each other."

God spreads them across the earth and they stop building. This city is called "Babel", where God confused the people.

"Make a name"

The builders should be vice-rulers, but they ignore God. They should fill the earth, but they stick together. God confuses and scatters them. Babel means "confused".

Why are God's punishments for the good of the people?

21

ACT 3: COVENANTS

SCENE 1: GOD'S PROMISES

Promising no more floods

God makes promises to help his spoiled world. Covenants are long-lasting agreements. Each promise has a reminder, like a ring at a wedding.

NOAH   ANIMALS   HUMANKIND

THE NOAHIC COVENANT

Never means never.

A Covenant of God • Directed by God
Produced by God • Written by God • Promised by God.

Reminder: Rainbow

★ ★ ★ ★ ★   ★ ★ ★ ★ ★

Movie Madness
"Hope to the hopeless. Brilliant."

Mesopotamian Mogul
"Rainbow eye candy. A great reminder to trust God."

"Everlasting covenant"

God promises never to flood the world again. He uses a rainbow to remind people of his patience. He will stick with his people, right to the end.

★ ★ ★ ★ ★

Why should humankind be glad about this covenant?

22

Promising land, nation, and blessing

God promises Abraham land, nation, and blessing. The Bible story is about how he keeps these promises. One descendant will defeat the devil: the snake crusher.

ABRAHAM   ABRAHAM'S DESCENDANTS

THE ABRAHAMIC COVENANT

Landowner. Father. Blessing for all.

"Blessing for all"
God will bless the whole world through Abraham's family line. People will live with God again, and God will bless them most as he defeats sin.

★ ★ ★ ★ ★

How will God bless the world through this covenant?

★ ★ ★ ★ ★
Haran Herald
"A blessing to watch! Abraham is unforgettable."

★ ★ ★ ★ ★
Mesopotamian Mogul
"Epic. We'll be watching this for the rest of time!"

Promising a special nation

Israel (Abraham's nation) is special because God chooses them. God also promises to make them different from other nations. Moses is their first leader at Mount Sinai.

MOSES   ISRAEL

THE MOSAIC COVENANT

At Mount Sinai, one question remains...
To obey or not to obey.

Reminder: **The Sabbath Day**

"Obey"
God is making Israel a different nation. Other nations have kings who set their laws. God wants Israel to obey his laws and to have a sabbath (rest) day to remind them.

★★★★★

How can Israel obey God?

★★★★★
The Assyrian Echo
"Jealous! No other nation has such good laws or a God so close."

★
The Moabite Times
"Israel is going nowhere. A flop waiting to happen."

Promising an eternal king

God promises King David a kingdom that will last forever. His kingdom will have a king who is the King of Kings, who will rule forever. He will be the "Son of David".

DAVID   AN ETERNAL KING

From the maker of "The Abrahamic Covenant"

THE DAVIDIC COVENANT

Bow before the King of Kings.

Babylonian Babble
"Bow before a nameless king? No way."

Arabian Express
"Unrealistic. Where can a king live forever?"

ASK POPCORN SALLY

Why are covenants so important?

God is super-committed to his people! Through the Bible we follow how God keeps his agreements, even when his people will not keep them.

"King of Kings"

A King of Kings from David's family line will rule forever. All peoples on earth will bow to a Son of David. There's no reminder for this covenant.

★ ★ ★ ★ ★

How does this covenant affect everyone?

SCENE 2: THE ABRAHAMIC COVENANT

Hello, Abram!

The promises to Abraham set the storyline for the Bible. Abraham becomes a Patriarch, the father of the people of Israel. But he's 75 years old and still childless!

CONTRACT
The Abrahamic Covenant

I do solemnly swear to give Abram everything below.

1. *Abram, I will give this land, the land of Canaan, to you and to your children after you. It is an everlasting gift from me.*

2. *I will make you into a great nation. I will multiply you, and you will father many nations. You are no longer called Abram, but Abraham, because you will father many. Even kings will come from you!*

3. *I will bless you and make your name great. And I will bless those who bless you, and curse those who curse you. I will bless all nations on earth through you.*

Abraham, walk with me with a clean heart. You and your descendants must all agree to keep my covenant.

Signed:
The Lord God Almighty

The Abrahamic Covenant Contract

<<< FLASHBACK

"Father of many"

Abraham means "father of many", and he will father nations. Since he trusts and obeys God, anyone who trusts and obeys him is his child too.

★ ★ ★ ★ ★

Sum up the three parts of the covenant.

… to the Tower of Babel (page 21). God promises Abraham a great name. It reminds us how the tower builders wanted a great name without God.

The smoking fire pot and flaming torch

Abraham wants help with trusting God's promises. How can he really know God will keep them? God knows Abraham's fears, and he vows to keep his promises.

CANAAN DIARY

Dear Diary,

God promised me a great land and nation. But I have no sons and this land is bare and barren. How can I trust God? So I asked him, "See, you have given me no children and someone who is not my son will be my heir."

God said, "Look up to the skies and count the stars. They are too many to count. This is how many children you will have." He also said, "I am the Lord and I am giving you this land to own." I asked him, "O Lord God, how can I know?"

God said, "Bring a young cow, goat, ram, turtledove, and pigeon. Cut the animals in half and lay them in a line, with the halves on different sides."

Then God put me in a deep sleep and explained, "Your children will suffer in a foreign land for 400 years, but I will save them and bring them back here."

A smoking fire pot and a flaming torch, representing God, passed between the animals. God promised: "Abraham, I really will give you this land, from the river of Egypt to the Euphrates, the land of many nations."

ASK 3D FREDDIE

Why does God choose Abraham?

You tell me! Abraham wasn't special! He probably worshipped the moon god until God called him. But God tells people to believe and he helps them to have faith.

"Made a covenant"

God swears to keep the Abrahamic Covenant. Often two people walked together between halved animals to swear on a promise, or die like the animals. God will keep this covenant by himself!

★ ★ ★ ★ ★

Why is God's promise so sure?

ACT 4: NATION ISRAEL

SCENE 1: GOD'S CAST FAMILY

A tale of two sons

Abraham has real faith. He believes God's promises and travels to Canaan with his wife, Sarah. They wait many years for the promised son, until Sarah comes up with a plan.

The Miracle Baby

1. Abraham makes Hagar the servant girl pregnant, but Sarah changes her mind about this plan.

2. Sarah hates Hagar and throws her out. An angel finds and comforts Hagar.

3. Angel: "Call your son Ishmael ('God hears') because God hears you."

4. Abraham holds Ishmael, his son. He is 86 years old!

5. The Lord: "Abraham, you will have a son by Sarah! Nations will come from her. Call him Isaac!"

6. Abraham: "How, Lord? I am NINETY-NINE!"

7. Sarah: "And how can I have this joy?" God: "Why did you laugh? Is anything too hard for me?"

8. Abraham: "Our promised Isaac, a miracle. Laughter in our old age!"

"Laughter"

God gives Abraham and Sarah laughter. First they laugh at his promise, then they laugh with happiness when Isaac is born. Isaac means "he laughs". The family continues!

★ ★ ★ ★ ★

FLASH-FORWARD >>>

… to Jesus' birth (page 100). Isaac and Jesus are both miracle babies. Sarah is 90 years old and Mary is a virgin when they have their sons.

Why is Isaac so important?

God tests Abraham

Abraham is raising Isaac to father the nation, but God tests his faith one last time. Will Abraham believe God's promises, even if it costs him his young son?

A Father's Sacrifice

1. The Lord asks Abraham to offer his only son as a sacrifice.

2. Abraham: "We will worship and both return."

3. Isaac: "Father, where's the lamb for the sacrifice?"

4. Abraham: "Isaac, my son, the Lord will provide."

5. Abraham is about to sacrifice Isaac.

6. Angel: "Stop! You obey fully by giving up your only son." Abraham turns and sees a ram from the Lord to sacrifice.

7. Abraham: "This place on Mount Moriah will be called 'The Lord will provide'."

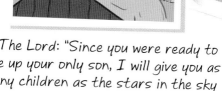

8. The Lord: "Since you were ready to give up your only son, I will give you as many children as the stars in the sky and the sand on the seashore."

FLASH-FORWARD >>>

… to the Cross (page 132). Three times God calls Isaac "your only son". God the Father will offer his only Son Jesus as a sacrifice on this same hill, 2,000 years later.

"The Lord will Provide"

Abraham discovers, again and again, that God provides. And God rewards his faith again and again. God will give him countless children, like the stars and the sand.

★ ★ ★ ★ ★

How does Abraham trust God?

Mission: find Isaac a wife!

Isaac has a problem. As Patriarch (father of the nation) he needs a wife! She must come from Haran, but Abraham is too old for the journey. Haran is 520 miles away!

Faith in Action

1. Isaac: "My oldest servant, find my son a wife from Haran. Swear you will do this."

2. The servant arrives, tired, and prays, "May the woman who gives me and my camels a drink be the wife chosen for Isaac."

3. Rebekah: "Drink, my lord. Your camels too!" Beautiful Rebekah offers water.

4. The servant looks at her in silence. He waits to learn God's plan.

5. The servant explains to brother Laban, "I feared she may not come, but Abraham said the Lord will prepare the way."

6. Laban and Rebekah's father say, "This all comes from the Lord. Take her!" They say goodbye to Rebekah for the last time.

7. Isaac is in the fields just as Rebekah is coming...

8. Rebekah: "Who is that man?" Love at first sight! They fall in love and marry; a match made in heaven.

"Chosen for Isaac"

Abraham and the servant expect God to choose a wife for Isaac. They have faith and pray for God's help. Rebekah and her family also accept the Lord's choosing.

★ ★ ★ ★ ★

FLASH-FORWARD >>>

... to Jacob in Haran (page 34). Jacob also comes to a well and finds a beautiful wife, Rachel.

How do Abraham and the servant show faith?

Struggling twins

Isaac shows faith like his father. Isaac and Rebekah cannot have children and he needs them to father the nation. He prays and God answers, but not as expected!

God's Surprising Choice

1. Isaac prays for a son. Rebekah is soon pregnant! Relief! But twins. Gasp!

2. The twins struggle and battle in Rebekah's womb. "HELP! Why is this happening to me?!"

3. The Lord: "Two nations struggle within you. This time the older will serve the younger."

4. Esau is blood red and hairy like a cloak. Jacob ("cheater") is holding Esau's heel.

5. Isaac prefers Esau the hunter and his meaty food. Rebekah prefers Jacob.

6. Esau: "I am starving! Give me some of that soup!" Jacob: "First sell me your birthright as the firstborn."

7. Esau: "I am DYING of hunger! My birthright can't help me now!"

8. Jacob: "Swear you will give me your rights!" Esau swears and swaps his birthright for some soup. He despises his birthright.

"Despises his birthright"

God chooses Jacob. The older Esau will serve the younger Jacob, because Esau doesn't care about his right to be chief. Jacob will lead, even though he's a cheater.

★ ★ ★ ★ ★

Why will Jacob lead the tribe?

FLASH-FORWARD ⟫⟫⟫

... to Jacob (page 32). Jacob means "cheater". He cheats his brother and will lie to his father. Later, his uncle cheats him back (page 34).

Isaac blesses Jacob

Jacob lives up to his name: "cheater". Isaac, old and blind, is ready to bless Esau and pass on God's promises to him. However, Jacob and Rebekah make a plan.

Cheated With Skins!

1. Isaac: "Esau, hunt and cook for me so I may bless you before I die."

2. Rebekah: "Jacob, let's make Isaac bless you!"

3. Rebekah goes to cook a tasty meal.

4. Rebekah dresses Jacob in Esau's clothes. She puts goat skins on his hands and neck. "I will take any curse for this!"

5. Isaac: "Are you really Esau? You sound like Jacob." "I am Esau," Jacob lies.

6. Isaac: "Then I bless you. Whoever curses you is cursed and whoever blesses you is blessed. Let nations bow to you."

7. Esau: "I am here, Father. Eat my food and bless me."

8. Isaac: "Who are you? Esau, I have blessed someone else! Your brother has cheated you."

<<< FLASHBACK

"Cheated"

Jacob is a massive cheater! He cheats his brother and father, and Isaac cannot take away the blessing. Now Jacob's descendants will bless the world.

★ ★ ★ ★ ★

… to Abraham (page 26). God also promised Abraham blessings to his people and curses to his enemies.

Why is the blessing important?

Jacob's dream

Jacob doesn't have his father's faith. He runs away to Haran, afraid for his future. Does God care about him? Will he return home? His mind whirls as he goes to sleep.

God's Same Promises

1. Jacob sleeps and dreams... A ladder reaches right up to heaven.

2. Angels climb up and down it and the Lord stands at the top.

3. "I am the Lord, the God of Abraham and Isaac."

4. "Your children will be like the dust of the earth. They will spread to the north, south, east, and west."

5. "I will bless all the families on earth through your children."

6. "I am with you and will keep you wherever you go."

7. "I will bring you back home one day."

8. Jacob: "The Lord is here. This stone marks this place: Bethel, the house of God."

"Like the dust"

God confirms that Jacob will lead the nation. He is Israel's third Patriarch. He will have more children than he can count, even after cheating Isaac and Esau so badly.

★ ★ ★ ★ ★

Why does Jacob have the dream?

FLASH-FORWARD >>>

... to Jesus' baptism (page 103). The ladder links heaven with earth, and Jesus links heaven and earth like a ladder (John 1:51). God calls Jesus his Son.

33

Jacob's new family

Jacob's uncle also plays tricks. Jacob arrives in Haran and finds his uncle Laban. Jacob begins to work for Laban and names his price – his beautiful daughter Rachel.

Two Weddings

1. Laban's elder daughter is droopy-eyed Leah. Laban's younger daughter is pretty Rachel.

2. Jacob: "I will work seven years for Rachel! A small time considering my love for her."

3. Jacob gets married. A happy day.

4. Jacob has been tricked. He has married Leah. An unhappy morning!

5. Laban: "Not the younger before the firstborn, Jacob!"

6. Laban: "You can marry Rachel if you work another seven years for me."

7. Jacob marries Rachel.

8. Jacob has twelve sons and a daughter.

"Not the younger before the firstborn"

Laban reminds Jacob of what he did to his brother Esau. Not the younger first here! Laban cheats Jacob out of seven more years. He's quite a match for Jacob.

★ ★ ★ ★ ★

FLASH-FORWARD >>>

… to Israel's twelve tribes (page 55). The tribes will be named after Jacob's sons.

How does Laban trick Jacob?

Jacob flees back home

Jacob has had enough. Laban cheats him for 20 years, so Jacob leaves secretly. But if he returns home, he must meet angry Esau! Jacob needs faith.

Three Meetings

1. Jacob's family flee without telling Laban, who is shearing sheep.

2. Laban: "I found you! Why have you tricked me? I could harm you, but God told me not to in a dream."

3. Jacob: "I worked twenty years for your daughters and sheep, but you changed my pay ten times! God saw and has told you off." Laban bids farewell.

4. Jacob waits by the River Jabbok and sees a mysterious man. Jacob wrestles with him until daybreak.

5. The man puts Jacob's hip out of joint, saying "Jacob, release me!" Jacob: "Only if you bless me!"

6. Man: "I rename you Israel because you struggled with God." Jacob: "I saw God's face and survived. I name this place Peniel ('the face of God')."

7. Esau runs to Jacob and offers him peace.

8. Israel: "Esau, seeing your face is like seeing the face of God. I have brought gifts for you. Take them. God has blessed me richly."

"Israel"

God changes Jacob. Jacob finally wants God's blessing! The man dislocates his hip to remind him how he struggled against God. Now he trusts God as his father had.

★ ★ ★ ★ ★

FLASH-FORWARD >>>

... to Israel's disobedience (pages 45, 49, 56–59, 71). Israel means "he struggles with God". The people of Israel will struggle between obeying and disobeying God.

How does God change Jacob?

Joseph and his dreams

Jacob repeats his father's mistakes. Isaac had preferred Esau, and now Jacob loves Joseph more than any of his sons, and he gives him a beautiful coat. Joseph becomes proud and boastful, and his brothers hate him.

Killing Off Joseph

1. Jacob makes Joseph a beautiful coat.

2. Joseph: "Hear my dream! We were binding sheaves of wheat and yours bowed to mine."

3. Brothers: "Excuse us! Do you think we will bow to you?"

4. Joseph: "Hear another dream! The sun, moon, and stars bowed to me."

5. Jacob: "Do you think we will all bow to you?"

6. Joseph travels many miles to join his brothers. He wants to fit in.

Brothers: "Here comes the dreamer! Let's kill him and say an animal did it."

7. The brothers sell Joseph to traders, who are on their way to Egypt.

8. They put blood on the coat and show Jacob. Jacob: "This is Joseph's! An animal has surely torn him to pieces. I will mourn until I die."

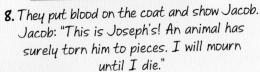

FLASH-FORWARD >>>

… to Joseph the ruler (page 39). Joseph's brothers will bow down to him, just like the sheaves of wheat. They won't realize what they are doing.

"The dreamer"

Joseph's brothers and father do not believe his dreams, which come from God. "Dreamer" is sarcastic. God uses their bad actions to save many people.

★ ★ ★ ★ ★

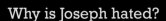

Why is Joseph hated?

Joseph the servant and prisoner

Joseph has been proud, and he must trust God. Joseph's name means "God increases", and God does bless him in Egypt! But God also allows him to suffer.

God Increases

1. Joseph works for Potiphar, a captain of Pharaoh's guard.

2. The Lord blesses Joseph's work. Potiphar makes him head servant and the Lord blesses Potiphar's home.

3. Potiphar's wife urges him every day, "Joseph, lie with me! Lie with me!"

4. Joseph: "No, my master has withheld nothing except you. How can I sin like this?" He runs but she rips his clothes and screams.

5. Potiphar sends Joseph to prison. The Lord blesses Joseph, and the jailer makes him head prisoner.

6. Pharoah's butler: "I dreamed a vine had three branches. I pressed its grapes into Pharaoh's cup." Joseph: "In three days you will be his cupbearer again. Remember me to him."

7. Pharaoh's baker: "I dreamed three bread baskets sat on my head, but birds ate the bread." Joseph: "In three days Pharaoh will behead you and birds will eat your body."

8. The butler and baker leave, but the butler forgets Joseph.

FLASH-FORWARD ⟩⟩⟩

… to Pharaoh's dreams (page 38). God has given Joseph a gift for explaining dreams, and this will soon be useful.

"The Lord blesses"

Joseph is learning that God is in charge. God blesses him, but also allows Joseph to suffer. God has a wider plan, and Joseph must trust him for rescue like the butler.

★ ★ ★ ★ ★

How does God bless Joseph?

37

Pharaoh's dreams

Joseph is a changed man. Two years later, Pharaoh has a dream and the butler remembers him. Joseph is now humble and he trusts God in good times and bad.

God Increases More

1. Joseph: "Pharaoh, you hear I can explain dreams. I cannot, but God will."

2. Pharaoh: "Seven fat cows came from the Nile and ate the reeds."

3. "Then seven thin cows came from the Nile. They came and ate the fat cows."

4. "I had a second dream. Seven big ears of grain sprouted together."

5. "Then seven withered ears came, scorched by the east wind, and swallowed them up!"

6. Joseph: "God shows you what he will do. The two dreams are one. Seven years of plenty will come, but seven years of famine will ruin Egypt."

7. "Pharaoh must choose a wise man to oversee Egypt. He must store a fifth of the grain in the good years to save Egypt in the bad years."

8. Pharaoh: "God's Spirit is in you! I set you over the whole land and you will be second only to me. Take my signet ring, robes, and chariot."

"God will make this happen"

Joseph now knows that only God increases. He has suffered, but God is in control. God gives the dreams and makes him ruler, to save many lives and bless the world.

★ ★ ★ ★ ★

FLASH-FORWARD >>>

… to Samson, Saul, and David (pages 59, 62, 63). Pharaoh sees that God gives Joseph special power. God's Spirit helps his people on special occasions!

How has God changed Joseph?

Joseph rules his brothers

Joseph the ruler has an opportunity. His brothers come to buy grain and bow without recognizing him. He will see if they are now honest men and trust God.

Saving Lives

1. Joseph: "You are spies!" Brothers: "No, we are twelve brothers. One is home and another is dead."

2. Joseph: "Prove it! Bring me the youngest! I will take a hostage."

3. Jacob is distraught and sends Benjamin, Rachel's second son. The brothers find their money put back in the grain sacks.

4. Brothers: "We found our money, and now bring double payment." Joseph: "Your God did that, I took your money! Is this your youngest?"

5. Joseph: "Feast now, go home tomorrow!" He seats them in age order, amazing them.

6. Before they leave, Joseph sneaks his silver cup into Benjamin's sack. Joseph's servants stop the brothers. "You stole the master's cup!" Brothers: "We didn't! Whoever did will die!" They find it in Benjamin's sack.

7. Judah: "Do not take the boy! It will kill our father! Take my life instead!"

8. Joseph reveals who he is. "I am Joseph, who you sold! Do not fear! You meant to harm me, but God meant it for good, to save many lives."

"God meant it for good"

Joseph knows that God can bring good from evil. He tells his brothers how God can use sufferings to create good. And it means he can forgive his brothers.

★ ★ ★ ★ ★

Why can Joseph forgive his brothers?

ASK POPCORN SALLY

Why do Abraham's family matter?

The stories of the family show us about faith in difficult times, and how God keeps his promises. He will not let his people go!

SCENE 2: GOD'S RESCUE

A hero is born!

Fast forward 400 years: God's people are slaves in Egypt. The Israelites (Hebrews) have multiplied in number, and Pharaoh fears for his safety. The Israelites pray for rescue.

PRINCESS PAMPERS

A HEBREW BABY was found yesterday on the banks of the Nile and a princess has taken him in, the EGYPTIAN SUN reports. Eyewitnesses say the baby was among the reeds. This baby is lucky to be alive – he must have a special life ahead of him.

Very recently Pharaoh ordered all Hebrew sons to be thrown into the Nile. Hebrew nurses can let newborn girls live, but must make Hebrew boys crocodile food. Reports say that the princess saw a basket among the reeds and found a three-month-old baby boy inside. The princess felt sorry for him and is expected to raise him as her own.

A Hebrew woman is nursing the baby. The gossip is that she is the baby's real mother. What is certain is that the boy is now Pharaoh's grandson, and the princess is calling him Moses, which means "drawn out" in Hebrew.

"Moses"
God plans his rescue through Moses, who is "drawn out". Pharaoh wanted to kill the boys in the Nile, but this is where rescue comes from. By his own daughter!

★ ★ ★ ★ ★

How is God a rescuer?

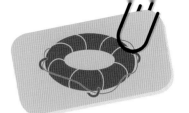

God speaks to Moses

A rescue seems impossible. Who can stop the misery? Moses, an Egyptian prince, saves a slave by killing a slave driver, then he flees to Midian. There he meets God…

GOD SPEAKS BURNING MESSAGE

MOSES, a long-term shepherd of Midian, says that God has spoken to him, and will now return to Egypt, the MIDIAN MAIL reports.

He says he came upon a burning bush on Mount Sinai, and heard the voice of God coming from it. He says the bush was on fire, but not burning up. The Bush Control Agency (BCA) call the sighting impossible.

Moses says God has seen his people's suffering and heard their prayers, and is sending Moses to ask for the release of the Hebrew slaves. Moses says this God calls himself "I AM WHO I AM". Moses will tell Pharaoh, "I AM has sent me to you. Release the slaves."

Moses says that God will rescue his people from slavery and bring them back to Mount Sinai. Moses claims God proved his power by turning his staff into a snake.

We at the MIDIAN MAIL wish him well on his rescue mission.

"I AM WHO I AM"

God uses his name to promise his rescue. "I AM WHO I AM" is also Yahweh, Lord, or Jehovah. It means he is all-powerful and eternal, and he will rescue with power.

★ ★ ★ ★ ★

Why should Moses trust God?

41

God shows power

Moses and his brother Aaron meet Pharaoh to pass on God's message. But he won't listen. He asks, "Who is your God?" God's power will teach him to listen.

EGYPT PLAGUED!

DOOM HAS HIT Egypt, the EGYPTIAN SUN reports, not just once but ten times. Everyone is asking, "Who is the God of Moses and Aaron?"

First, the Nile became blood. Fish died and we could not drink. Then frogs infested our beds, ovens, and food. Next gnats came and we scratched away, before flies swarmed over Egypt, never buzzing off! Then our livestock died. Then boils festered on us. This was followed by hail devastating our crops. Locusts then devoured everything left behind, before darkness made us fear for three days.

Lastly, our firstborn sons died and we wailed. Pharaoh has released those slaves and maybe our suffering is over.

FLASH-FORWARD >>>

… to the Cross (page 132). The Hebrews trust the lamb's blood for rescue, and Jesus saves anyone who trusts his sacrifice for rescue.

SAVED BY LAMBS!

A PASSOVER has saved our firstborn sons, the HEBREW EXPRESS briefly reports.

Last night "I AM" came to kill. But he told us to sacrifice lambs and smear their blood on our doors. When he saw the blood, he passed over our homes. We will remember this Passover forever. This is our last report; today we are free!

"Passover"

God's rescue is for Hebrews and Egyptians. The blood on the doors saves many from death and God will pass over their homes. They must trust the blood of the lamb.

★ ★ ★ ★ ★

How does God rescue his people?

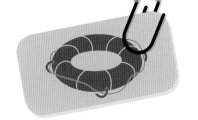

God's great rescue

God soon shows his power unforgettably. About 2 million Hebrews leave Egypt as an exodus (mass exit), but Pharaoh changes his mind and gives chase.

MILLIONS WALK THROUGH SEA TO FREEDOM

THE RED SEA parted for the exodus, the MIDIAN MAIL reports. Eyewitnesses say the slaves walked through on dry ground, with walls of water on their right and left, before it closed on the chasing army.

Moses explains God said, "The Egyptians will know I am the Lord as I show my glory."

Moses lifted his staff and a strong wind divided the waters. The terrified Hebrews crossed, chased by the Egyptian chariots. On the other side, Moses stretched out his hand again and the waters covered the Egyptian chariots and horsemen.

Egypt and many other nations have heard of this God and the sea crossing. Life insurance claims are set to flood the army's offices.

The Hebrews have seen the Lord's power and fear him. What else can this God do?

"The Egyptians will know"

God wants the world to know his power. News spreads to Egypt and many other nations that "I AM" is the true God and Israel is his special nation.

★ ★ ★ ★ ★

Why does God part the Red Sea?

ASK 3D FREDDIE

Was the Red Sea at low tide?

Not a chance! Tides don't produce walls of water! The Red Sea was very deep, and the Egyptians would not have been drowned by a killer tide!

SCENE 3: GOD'S SPECIAL EFFECTS

God makes Israel special

God has three blessings for Israel. His gifts will help them to obey him in the Promised Land. At Mount Sinai, he firstly tells Israel who they are and how to live.

BLESSING 1: LAW

Visuals and Sounds

Mount Sinai trembles

Thick smoke

Lightning

Long trumpet blast, getting louder

Thunder sounds

Rumbling sounds

Voiceover

"Israel, I saved you on eagles' wings and brought you to me.

"Now obey me fully and keep my covenant, my serious agreement with you.

"Then I will treasure you above any other nation. You will be a holy nation."

Props: Ten Commandments

"I am the Lord who rescued you from Egypt. Have no other gods but me."

"Do not make idols."

"Do not misuse my name."

"Keep the sabbath separate for rest."

"Respect your parents."

"Do not murder."

"Do not be unfaithful in marriage."

"Do not steal."

"Do not tell lies."

"Do not long for what is not yours."

"Holy nation"

Holy means "different and special". God tells Israel they are separate from all other nations. God has saved them alone! They must obey the Law to live differently.

★ ★ ★ ★ ★

How is Israel special?

God feeds Israel

Aaron and Israel quickly forget God. Aaron is their high priest and Moses is up the mountain with God. God blesses them, but they want a god they can see.

Designs for Israel

Prop 1: Manna

Honey wafer bread

Appears every morning

Designed by the Lord

Prop 2: Running Water

Constant fresh drinking water

Flows from a desert rock

Designed by the Lord

Prop 3: Golden Calf

Lump of metal

Melted from golden jewels

Designed by Aaron

"Israel, these are your gods who rescued you from Egypt."

Prop 4: Altar

Pile of stones

For offerings to the calf

Designed by Aaron

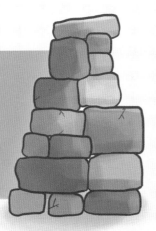

"These are your gods"

Aaron and Israel want gods they can see and control. They act like the other nations and build a golden calf. They don't know and trust God, even after he rescued them.

★ ★ ★ ★ ★

Why does Israel build the calf?

God lives in the camp

God has a plan to live with his people. He rules them by the Ten Commandments, kept in the ark of the covenant, and now they must build a tent for meeting God.

BLESSING 2: THE TABERNACLE

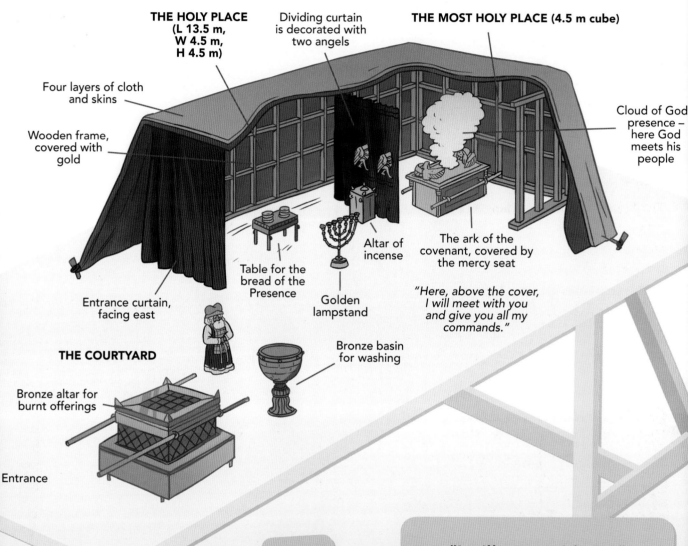

THE HOLY PLACE (L 13.5 m, W 4.5 m, H 4.5 m)

Dividing curtain is decorated with two angels

THE MOST HOLY PLACE (4.5 m cube)

Four layers of cloth and skins

Wooden frame, covered with gold

Cloud of God presence – here God meets his people

Entrance curtain, facing east

Table for the bread of the Presence

Altar of incense

Golden lampstand

The ark of the covenant, covered by the mercy seat

"Here, above the cover, I will meet with you and give you all my commands."

THE COURTYARD

Bronze basin for washing

Bronze altar for burnt offerings

Entrance

<<< FLASHBACK

... to Eden (page 17). The angels on the east-facing curtain are like the angels guarding Eden. God lives with his people in the Most Holy Place.

"I will meet with you"

God lives in the portable tent. A cloud of his glory fills the tabernacle's Most Holy Place, above the ark of the covenant. He saves his people to live with them.

★ ★ ★ ★ ★

What is the tabernacle for?

Payments for sin

Israel still has a problem. Their sin cuts them off from living with God, so he gives them sacrifices to pay for their sin. Every year they have a Day of Atonement.

BLESSING 3: SACRIFICES

The Goat for Sacrifice

The high priest takes two male goats and kills one.

He sprinkles the goat's blood on the mercy seat seven times.

The goat dies in the place of the people.

The Scapegoat

The high priest lays his hands on the other goat's head.

He confesses Israel's sins and sends the goat far into the desert.

The scapegoat takes the blame far away from the people.

"The animal's life is in the blood. Blood makes atonement for a life."

ASK POPCORN SALLY

Do the sacrifices make Israel perfect?

Sadly not. Animals cannot pay for humans, but they fill a gap until a perfect sacrifice fully pays for sins. That's Jesus, about 1,500 years later.

"Life is in the blood"

One life pays for another. This is atonement. One animal dies in the place of Israel, and the other one carries their guilt away into the desert. The people can only live with God if they are clean of sin.

★ ★ ★ ★ ★

How do sacrifices help?

FLASH-FORWARD >>>

… to the Cross (page 132). The goat dies for Israel once per year, and Jesus dies for his people once for all time.

SCENE 4: GOD'S LOCATION SCOUT

Israel scouts Canaan

The Promised Land is Israel's for the taking. God tells Moses to choose twelve spies to scout out Canaan's food and people. Their journey covers about 500 miles.

MISSION REPORT

1 **Moses** Go, spy out our land! See who lives there, strong, weak, few, or many.

2 **Moses** Tell us about their cities. Are they unwalled or fortified?

3 **Moses** Study the land. How fertile is the soil? And bring back some fruit.

4 *(Twelve spies explore the land for 40 days, and return with lots of fruit.)*

5 **12 Spies** The land flows with milk and honey! Here, see some of its fruit!

6 **12 Spies** But its people are strong and their cities are well-fortified!

7 **Joshua and Caleb** We're Joshua and Caleb and we say the land is ours for the taking. God has promised it. We can certainly win!

8 **10 Spies** No, we can't! They are so strong, we were like grasshoppers compared to them!

"Milk and honey"

Israel forgets God. The spies see cows, bees, fruit, and giants, but they soon forget God's power seen in the plagues, the Red Sea, and at Sinai. They fear the Canaanites, not God.

★ ★ ★ ★ ★

Why should the spies trust God?

48

Israel rebels

Grumbling Israel still doubts God. The ten spies tell Israel about the giants, and the people complain about leaving Egypt. Joshua and Caleb remind them about God.

MERCY AND JUSTICE

1 **Israel** Let's go back to Egypt and not die in Canaan. Those giants will slaughter our children!

2 **Israel** Let's have a new leader. Not Moses!

3 **Joshua and Caleb** God will lead us to the land and give it to us! It flows with milk and honey!

4 **Joshua and Caleb** Do not rebel against the Lord. And don't fear those people. God says it's our land!

5 **The Lord** Moses, they call me worthless after all I have done. I will strike them down.

6 **Moses** Lord, the Egyptians will hear! After you saved us from them! Forgive our people as you have done until now.

7 **The Lord** Moses, I will forgive them. But they won't see the land. They will wander in the desert for 40 years, near the Red Sea.

8 **The Lord** From these people, only Joshua and Caleb will enter the land now. Your children, who you feared for, will see the land.

"I will forgive"

God is merciful and forgives, but he also gives Israel what they ask for. They can return toward Egypt and die in the desert. Their children will enter Canaan instead.

★ ★ ★ ★ ★

What does Israel need to remember about God?

The bronze snake

God teaches Israel to depend on him. They must pick food from the ground every day – honey bread (manna) and quail – and also trust him with their lives.

A WAY OUT OF DEATH

1 Israel God and Moses! Why did you bring us from Egypt to die here?

2 Israel We have no bread. We have no water. And we hate this food!

3 *(The Lord sends poisonous snakes.)*

4 *(They bite many Israelites and many die.)*

5 Israel We sinned against the Lord and you! Moses, pray God takes away these horrible snakes!

6 The Lord Moses, make a snake and put it on a pole. Then whoever looks up at it will live.

7 *(Moses makes a bronze snake and lifts it up high.)*

8 *(When the bitten people look up at the snake, they live.)*

FLASH-FORWARD ⋙

… to the Cross (page 132). The bronze snake gives life, but Jesus promises eternal life. He is put on a cross for all to see.

"We sinned"

The bronze snake makes Israel act in faith and look up. God saves their lives as mercifully as he provides food. Their complaining must stop!

★ ★ ★ ★ ★

How does the bronze snake help Israel?

Moses' last instructions

Israel must be better than their parents when they enter Canaan. 40 years later, Moses gives a final speech before going to die on Mount Nebo, aged 120.

HOW TO LIVE IN CANAAN

- Both people treasured by the Lord
- Both chosen out of all the nations on earth

Blessings

- Respects the Lord God
- Obeys the Lord God
- Loves the Lord God

Blessings to Follow:
1. Many children
2. Much fruit and food
3. Many victories over enemies

Curses

- Does not obey the Lord God
- Intermarries with foreigners so his heart turns away from the Lord God

Curses to Follow:
1. Few children
2. Bad fruit and food
3. Many defeats by enemies

ASK 3D FREDDIE

Why would anyone disobey?

That's sin! People's heads might know what's right, but their hearts choose what they feel like. They should remember God's blessings and thank him every day.

"Blessings and curses"

God cares if Israel obeys. He treasures them as different and they must live differently. His blessings and curses offer greater reason to obey!

★ ★ ★ ★ ★

How and why must Israel obey God?

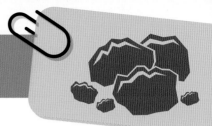

SCENE 5: GOD'S STAGE

Joshua leads

It's time Israel began conquering! God chooses Joshua as Israel's new leader. The city of Jericho has heard that God will turn its walls to rubble. Rahab, who lives there, helps Israel.

RAHAB'S FAITH

Joshua: *(boldly)* You two! Go and spy out Canaan, especially Jericho.

(The spies arrive and are discovered!)

Spies: *(urgently)* Excuse me, let us in! Men are chasing us! Hide us!

Rahab: *(quickly)* Of course – hide on the roof under the flax.

King: *(loudly)* Tell Rahab: "where are those men? They are spies!"

Soldiers: *(angrily)* Rahab, where are those men? They are spies!

Rahab: The men were here… I didn't know who they were, but they left at dusk before the gates closed. Go quickly!

(The soldiers leave and run out of the city gates.)

Rahab: *(to the spies)* I know the Lord has given you the land. All our people melt in fear! We hear how the Lord even parted the Red Sea for you. Swear by the Lord you will show kindness to my family and will not kill us!

Spies: We swear! Our lives for your lives! You must keep our secret too!

Rahab: Go to the hills and hide for three days, then go on your way!

Spies: Tie this red cord to your window and bring your family into your house. You will be responsible if anyone dies outside your house. We will be responsible if anyone inside your house dies. Now keep our secret!

Rahab: Agreed. Just as you say. I'm tying it right now! *(Ties the cord)*

(The spies climb down a rope and run for the hills, then to Joshua.)

Spies: Joshua, the Lord has given us the land and its people are melting in fear!

"I know"

Rahab has faith. She believes in God's power and speaks bravely to the soldiers. She knows God's power and wants to join Israel.

★ ★ ★ ★ ★

How does Rahab show faith?

<<< FLASHBACK

… to Passover (page 42). The scarlet red cord echoes the lamb's blood on the doors. The look of blood saves Rahab.

Crossing the Jordan

Israel's journey from Egypt is over! They stand by the River Jordan, ready to cross. But the land promised to Abraham is blocked and there's no bridge!

ENTERING BY A MIRACLE

Officers: *(to the people)* Follow the priests.

Joshua: *(to the people)* Tomorrow the Lord will do amazing things!

Joshua: *(to the priests)* Carry the ark ahead of the people.

The Lord: *(to Joshua)* Tell the priests to stand in the shallows of the river.

Joshua: *(to the people)* When the ark touches the river, the Lord will stop its water.

(The priests carry the ark to the edge of the river waters.)

(The water stops upstream, piling up high.)

(The priests wait in the middle of the river.)

(The nation of Israel passes over opposite Jericho.)

(40,000 armed soldiers march over.)

The Lord: *(to Joshua)* Twelve men must collect a stone from the river.

(Twelve men collect and carry across a stone.)

The Lord: *(to Joshua)* Tell the priests carrying the ark to finish their crossing.

Joshua: *(to the priests)* Come up out of the Jordan.

(The priests cross over and the water begins to flow again.)

(Joshua piles up the twelve stones as a memorial.)

Joshua: *(to the people)* When your children ask, "What do these stones mean?" tell them, "Here is where Israel crossed the Jordan on dry ground." The Lord dried up the Jordan just like the Red Sea, to show you his great power so you respect him."

(In nearby countries, the kings' hearts melt in fear...)

"The nation"

Israel enters the Promised Land just how they left Egypt. God parts the River Jordan like the Red Sea, and Israel is called a nation for the first time. Home at last!

★ ★ ★ ★ ★

Why is Joshua a good leader?

Smashing Jericho!

Israel must act out their faith. They approach Jericho's thick walls, knowing that only God can turn them to rubble. Israel and God will act together.

WORKING WITH GOD

The Lord: *(to Joshua)* I am giving you Jericho and its fighting men. March around its walls once per day, for six days. Carry the ark at the front, with priests blowing trumpets. On day seven, circle the city seven times. Blow a long trumpet blast and tell the army to shout. Jericho's walls will fall and you may attack.

Joshua: *(to the priests)* Carry the ark around the city, and blow trumpets!

Joshua: *(to the army)* March around the city, behind the ark!

(The priests carry the ark, and some blow trumpets.)

(The army marches around Jericho.)

(They do this once per day, for six days.)

Joshua: *(to the priests and army)* Today, circle the city seven times.

(The priests and army circle Jericho seven times.)

(Then the priests blow a long trumpet blast.)

Joshua: *(to the army)* Shout! The Lord has given you the city! Spare Rahab!

(The army shouts. The city walls collapse and everyone charges in.)

(The army kill men and women, cattle, sheep, and donkeys.)

Joshua: *(to the spies)* Bring out Rahab and her family. Make them safe outside.

(The army burn the city and save its precious metals.)

Joshua: *(to everyone)* Cursed is anyone who rebuilds Jericho's walls. He who lays its foundations will lose his first son, and whoever builds its gates will lose his last.

(Joshua's reputation spreads across all the lands...)

"The Lord has given you"

God acts as Israel acts. They look strange circling the city, but they remember God's promises to Abraham, Isaac, and Jacob. They obey and God gives them the land.

★ ★ ★ ★ ★

How do God and Israel act together?

ASK POPCORN SALLY

Who conquers? God or Israel?

Both together! While they obey, God provides. He even stops the sun so they can finish a battle in daylight! They can't do that. At least, I can't!

Geography: Israel's Journey

God's new nation has covered thousands of miles. They have had great leaders and defeated great kingdoms. They cover Israel, Egypt, Saudi Arabia, and Jordan.

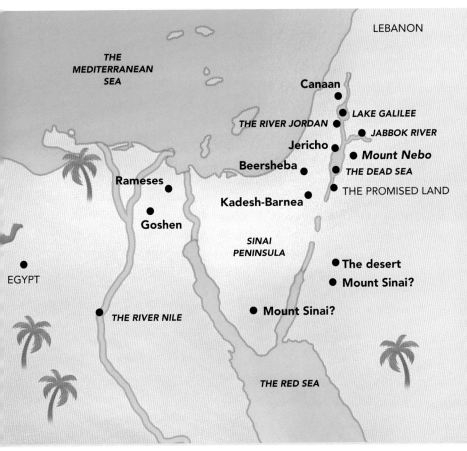

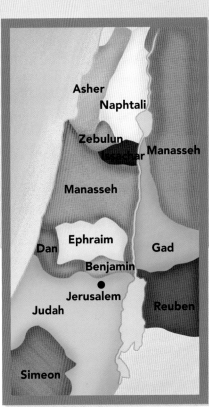

Areas given to the twelve tribes of Israel

*Maps not to scale

- **Beersheba** was Abraham's home. Jacob lived in Bethel, just north toward Haran.

- **Jabbok River** was where Jacob wrestled with God.

- **Egypt** was ruled by Joseph at the peak of its power (c.1900–1730 BC).

- **The River Nile** often floods and saves Egypt from famines more than it saves other nations.

- **Goshen** was home to the Hebrews after Joseph became ruler.

- **Rameses** was a city built by Israelite slaves for Pharaoh Rameses.

- **The Red Sea** forked around the **Sinai Peninsula.**

- **Mount Sinai** may be Jebel Musa on the peninsula, or Jebel al-Lawz in Saudi Arabia.

- **Kadesh-Barnea** was the base from which Moses sent his twelve spies.

- **The desert** on the way to the Red Sea was home to Israel for 40 years.

- **Canaan** was home to the mighty Canaanites.

- **The Promised Land** swept from the Nile to the Euphrates, Lebanon to the desert.

- **Mount Nebo** was where Moses died, overlooking the Promised Land.

- **The River Jordan** runs from Lake Galilee to **The Dead Sea**.

- **Jericho** was conquered first by Joshua. Historians say it was founded around 9000 BC.

SCENE 6: GOD'S JUDGES

Ehud kills King Eglon

After Joshua, Israel forgets God's deeds. Israel spares the Canaanites and worships their gods, so God brings foreign kings. Israel prays for rescuing leaders: judges!

BEST
LEFTY

EHUD

"Left-handed man"
God rescues Israel with an unlikely man. The Moabites assume Ehud is right-handed and check the wrong side for a sword. Bold Ehud then rules Israel for 80 years.

★ ★ ★ ★ ★

Why does God send judges?

ACCEPTANCE SPEECH

We prayed and God provided! We served King Eglon of Moab for 18 years, but the Lord heard our prayers and gave us... me, Ehud!

Thank you for this award. Let me tell you what I did. One day some of us went to offer gifts to Eglon. I'm a left-handed man and I strapped a short sword to my right thigh, under my clothes. We gave our gifts to Eglon and left. But after a few minutes, I went back to Eglon and told him I had a secret message for him.

Eglon was a very fat man! He sent out his servants and I said, "My message is from God!" I pulled out my sword and thrust it into his fat belly! I pushed it so hard that the hilt of the sword went in after the blade and he even pooed himself!

I left and locked the room. The servants did not enter because they thought Eglon was going for a poo (which he was!). Later on, they found him dead on the floor.

Soon I returned with soldiers. That day we killed 10,000 strong Moabites! None survived. Thanks to the Lord for giving us strength and for choosing me, a lefty!

Deborah advises Barak

Israel soon worships foreign gods again. So God brings Jabin and Sisera, the Canaanite king and army commander. After 20 years, Israel prays again for help.

ACCEPTANCE SPEECH

Thank you! Wow! God heard our prayers. Jabin and Sisera had terrorized us for 20 years, but God gave us the victory.

Each day I sat by a palm tree advising people. I sent for Barak and gave him the Lord's messages: "God will help you beat Sisera. Gather 10,000 men to fight!" But Barak didn't trust God. He pleaded, "Only if you go with me!" Because of this, God said a woman would kill Sisera. The glory will go to her, not to Barak.

I joined Barak and his 10,000 men, and we faced Sisera's 900 iron chariots and army. "Go, Barak, the Lord goes before you!" So Barak destroyed Sisera's army and Sisera fled on foot. He came to a woman called Jael expecting safety!

Jael hid Sisera under a rug in her tent. She gave him milk when he asked for water and he fell fast asleep. And she took a tent peg and drove it through his head. Messy! God used two women to beat Jabin and his armies. I dedicate this to Jael, stronger than Sisera and braver than Barak. To her!

BEST SUPPORTING LADY

DEBORAH

"Go with me!"

Barak looks for support in the wrong places. He trusts Deborah more than God, and the glory goes to a housewife called Jael. Then God gives Israel rest for 40 years.

★ ★ ★ ★ ★

Why does Jael get Barak's glory?

ASK 3D FREDDIE
What are the judges for?

Leading! For 200 to 300 years, Israel does whatever it wants and God brings enemies to make his people turn to him again. God is both a punisher and a rescuer.

Gideon and his 300 men

Soon Israel turns away from God again. So God brings the Midianites like locusts, eating Israel's food for seven years. Israel prays again for a strong rescuer…

BEST WEAKLING

GIDEON

"I will be with you!"

Weak Gideon must trust God for strength. God promises to fight for him, and his tiny army even defeat the Midianites without weapons! Gideon rules for 40 years.

★ ★ ★ ★ ★

Why is Gideon's victory so easy?

ACCEPTANCE SPEECH

Best WEAKLING?! Oh. I guess that's true though. An angel of the Lord told me, "The Lord is with you, O man of courage! Save Israel, I am sending you!" I said, "How can I? My people are the weakest in our tribe, and I am the weakest in my family!" But the Lord said, "I will be with you!"

My trust in God was weaker so I kept begging for signs. I asked God for dew to land only on a woollen fleece. When he did it, I asked again!

God wanted our numbers to be weak! We had 32,000 men but I had to send away any who were afraid. 22,000 left! God said there were still too many! He sent us to the river. Any who used their hands to drink from it will fight, and any who drank like dogs had to leave. After that, only 300 men were left! Smallest. Army. Ever.

That night everyone carried a trumpet and a flaming torch in a jar. We surrounded the Midianites and blew the trumpets and smashed the jars. "A sword for the Lord and for Gideon!" we screamed. Down below, the Midianites panicked and killed each other! We chased them and finished them off! This award is for weaklings who trust God!

Samson and Delilah

Israel is unfaithful again. So God brings the Philistines to rule for 40 years and soon Israel prays. God gives them Samson, a judge with huge strength, but Samson is unfaithful too!

ACCEPTANCE SPEECH

Thanks babes. But no thanks to my wife Delilah, who made me blind and alone. When I was born, an angel gave me three rules. But I haven't been good...

1) No touching dead bodies. One day a lion attacked me. God's Spirit gave me strength and I tore it to pieces like a young goat. Later on, I found a beehive in the dead lion. Yum! Honey! Another time I burned the Philistines' wheat fields down. I tied 300 foxes' tails together, with torches in each knot. God's Spirit strengthened me and I killed 1000 men with a dead donkey's jawbone.

2) No wine. But in that time, I got married and feasted and drank wine heavily. For a week! Then those Philistines killed my wife because I burned their fields. Grrr.

3) No haircuts. I married Delilah, a Philistine. Her people used her to find out the secret of my strength. I lied three times but she broke my heart. "Samson, if you love me, you will tell me!" I told her that if my hair is cut, my strength will go. That night she cut my hair and the Philistines gouged out my eyes.

But my hair is back! They now mock me in their temple, and I have prayed, "Lord, strengthen me once more so I can avenge them for my eyes. Let me die with them!" I will pull down their temple and kill more in my death than in my whole life. Run!

BEST THUG

SAMSON

"God's Spirit"
God generously uses unfaithful people. He gives Samson superhuman strength, even though he is a rule-breaker. Samson judges Israel for 20 years.

★ ★ ★ ★ ★

How does Samson break the rules?

Ruth joins Naomi

Naomi needs help. During the time of the judges, Naomi and her husband Elimelech go from Bethlehem to Moab. Their sons marry Moabites, but her husband and sons die.

BEST FOREIGNER

RUTH

"Your people... and your God"

Ruth joins Naomi's people and God. She gives up her life in Moab for a new family and God in Bethlehem. God rescues her under his wings, a sign of his rescue.

★ ★ ★ ★ ★

Why is Boaz so kind to Ruth?

ACCEPTANCE SPEECH

I could not leave Naomi! I married her son, but when he died she told me to find a new husband. She begged, "Your sister-in-law has gone back to her people and her gods. Go too!"

I'm a Moabite, but I could not leave her. "Wherever you go I will go. Wherever you stay I will stay. Your people will be my people, and your God will be my God. I will die where you die. May God punish me if anything but death separates us."

In Bethlehem, people saw us. "Naomi and Ruth the Moabite!" I went to glean in the fields, to gather grain left by the reapers. By chance, I was in the field of Boaz, a relative of Elimelech. He said, "Listen, my daughter, do not glean anywhere else. You will be safe."

Boaz was so kind! He knew I came to Bethlehem with Naomi and said, "May the Lord fully repay your kindness, since you have come here under his wings."

He cared for me, even though I was not his servant. Any award should go to him! He sat me by his reapers at lunchtime and gave me food. Enough to fill me! He even gave me grain from his reapers' bundles! I gleaned in his fields every day, and Naomi explained who Boaz was...

Boaz redeems Ruth

Naomi hopes for a rescue. Boaz is a redeemer, a relative who can "buy back" Ruth. Boaz can marry Ruth and continue Elimelech's family line. Boaz can be a rescuer.

ACCEPTANCE SPEECH

One night, as I slept, I found Ruth at my feet. Dear Naomi sent her. She uncovered my feet and waited for me to wake. She said the sweetest words. "I am Ruth, your maidservant. Spread your robe like wings over me. You are a redeemer."

Ruth wanted to give Naomi a new family! Any award should go to her! I told her, "Do not fear, you are a worthy woman and I am a redeemer. But there is a redeemer nearer in line than me. I will redeem you if he will not. Tomorrow I will find out."

I met the relative and gathered ten elders. "Naomi has returned from Moab and is selling some of Elimelech's land. Buy it, or I will redeem it because I come after you."

My relative said, "I will redeem it." But I explained, "When you buy the land, you also get Ruth. She is a Moabite widow and you will have to continue Elimelech's family line with her." He did not want to marry Ruth and so gave her to me. We agreed in front of the witnesses, and I took Ruth as my wife, to continue Naomi's family line.

We married! The city praised God because I redeemed Ruth, and we had a son. Naomi nursed the boy and we named him Obed. He will name his son Jesse.

BEST REDEEMER

BOAZ

"Redeemer"

Boaz redeems Ruth. He "buys her back", and spreads his wings over (rescues) her. He will give them a new family. As Ruth hoped, Naomi's people will be her people.

★ ★ ★ ★ ★

FLASH-FORWARD ⟫⟫

… to the Cross (page 132). Boaz kindly redeems Ruth and Naomi, "buying them back" into his family. Jesus, also from Bethlehem, redeems his people to live with God.

How does Boaz redeem Ruth?

SCENE 7: GOD'S KINGS

King Saul does what he wants

Israel is jealous of the nations around it. After 200 to 300 years of judges, they demand a king to lead. But their prophet Samuel warns them: kings rule for themselves, not for God!

A WAY OUT OF DEATH

1 **Samuel** Saul, the Lord anoints you, choosing you as king. *(God's Spirit rushes on Saul.)*

2 **Israel** Long live Saul! Long live the king! He is a head taller than anyone!

3 *(God's Spirit rushes on Saul. He cuts cattle in half.)*

4 **Saul** Whoever does not follow Samuel and me to battle will die like these cattle! Let's take 300,000 men to defeat the Ammonites.

5 **Samuel** *(Much later…)* Saul, attack the Amalekites. Spare no one, but destroy their people and all their animals.

6 **Saul and Nation** *(After defeating the Amalekites)* Come, let's spare King Agag and keep his best sheep and cattle for a sacrifice.

7 **Samuel** *(To Saul)* Why have you not obeyed the Lord?
Saul I did! We only spared their king, and their cattle for a sacrifice.
Samuel As king, you must obey! To obey is better than sacrifice.

8 **Saul** I have sinned. I obeyed the people, not the Lord.
Samuel *(Saul grabs Samuel's robe; it tears.)* The Lord has torn your kingdom from you and will give it to another man.

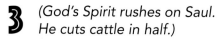

"To obey is better"

Saul fails to obey God and makes excuses. Kings must set the example, and God cares more about obedience than sacrifices. He will tear away Saul's kingdom.

★ ★ ★ ★ ★

How does Saul disobey God?

Samuel anoints David

Israel needs a godly king: one who loves God from the heart. God sends Samuel to Jesse of Bethlehem to anoint (choose) a king. God's choice will surprise Samuel.

GOD'S CHOICE

1 **Samuel** *(Meets Jesse)* I am here to sacrifice. I invite you and your sons to join me.

2 **Samuel** *(Sees Eliab; looks strong)* Surely this is God's new king?

3 **The Lord** Samuel, do not look at the outside. The Lord sees differently from humans. People look at the outside appearance, but the Lord looks at the heart.

4 **Samuel** *(Seven sons pass Samuel)* Perhaps the king will be Abinadab? Shammah? One of the others?

5 **Samuel** *(Concerned)* Do you have any more sons? **Jesse** *(Thinks)* The youngest is out tending sheep. He is a shepherd.

6 **David** *(Arrives glowing with health, handsome and fine.)* I'm home!

7 **The Lord** Samuel, anoint David with a horn of oil. He is the one.

8 *(Samuel anoints him in front of his brothers and God's Spirit rushes on him.)*

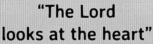

FLASH-FORWARD ▷▷▷

... to Bethlehem (page 99). David's greater descendant is also born in Bethlehem. Jesus will shepherd his people.

"The Lord looks at the heart"

God and Israel see differently. David is a shepherd boy, but will be a good king. His heart loves God first, and Israel needs a king who will shepherd them to obey.

★ ★ ★ ★ ★

What kind of king does God want?

David and Goliath

Israel will soon see God's choice of king. They go to battle with the Philistines and, for 40 days, a giant challenges God's nation. David will soon be famous…

A FAMOUS VICTORY

1 **Goliath** *(3 metres tall, shouts war cry)* Give me a man to fight me! If he wins, we will be your servants!

2 **David** *(Arrives with food for his brothers)* Who is he? How dare he challenge the Lord! Saul, I was a shepherd and I fought lions and bears. This man is no different. Allow me to fight him. He has challenged the armies of the living God.

3 **Saul** *(Putting armour on him)* Go, and may God go with you. Wear my armour.

4 **David** *(Weighed down)* I cannot! I am not used to this. I will just take five stones and my sling.

5 **Goliath** Am I a dog that you come at me with sticks? I curse you by my gods.

6 **David** I come to you in the name of the Lord Almighty! The whole world will know that there is a God in Israel and he does not save with sword and spear. He now hands you over to us. *(Slings a stone at Goliath)*

7 *(The stone lodges in Goliath's head. David runs to Goliath, takes his sword and chops off his head. The Philistines flee and Israelites attack.)*

8 **Saul** *(To David)* Whose son are you?
David My father is Jesse, from Bethlehem.

"The whole world will know"

God uses David to rescue Israel. Goliath is 3 m tall and his armour weighs 55 kg, but a small shepherd boy defeats him with a single stone! The world knows this story!

★ ★ ★ ★ ★

How does David trust God?

King Saul wants David dead

David becomes a godly general. The people cheer, "Saul has killed thousands and David has killed tens of thousands." Saul hates David, but David still respects Saul.

RESPECTING GOD'S CHOICE

1 **Saul** *(Throws spear at David)* Agghhhh! I'll pin David to the wall! *(David dodges and runs.)*
Jonathan David, run for your life. My father will kill you. Go, before it is too late!

2 *(Saul chases David into the hills with 3000 men. He goes into a cave for a bathroom break.)*

3 **David's Men** See, here is your moment. David, kill him before he kills you!

4 *(David nears Saul and cuts a corner off his robe.)*
David What am I doing? The Lord forbid I harm the Lord's anointed. He is God's choice! Men, you must not harm him either.

5 **David** *(Saul leaves cave.)* Saul, why do you think I want to kill you? I will not kill the Lord's anointed! He handed you to me, but I cut off a corner of your robe. May the Lord judge between us. I will not kill his anointed!
Saul *(Weeps)* You are better than me. The Lord handed me to you but you let me live. Now I know you will be king. Swear to spare my children after me!

6 *(Later, in battle, Philistines kill Saul's sons and hit Saul with arrow.)*

7 **Saul** Armour bearer, kill me with your sword!
Armour bearer *(Trembling)* I cannot!
Saul Then I must. *(Falls on his own sword. Philistines win and Israel mourns.)*

8 *(Philistines find Saul's body, cut off head, take armour, and spread the news.)*

"The Lord's anointed one"

David cares more about obedience than power. God chose Saul too, and David will not rush his way to the throne. His love and obedience will make him a good king.

★ ★ ★ ★ ★

Why does David spare Saul's life?

King David's highs

David really loves God. He's a "man after God's heart". He becomes king and sets an example for his people to love and obey God too. His name will go down in history.

INTERVIEW SPECIAL!
3D FREDDIE MEETS KING DAVID

3D Freddie: David! It's a pleasure to meet you! How did you become king?

King David: The people anointed me king when I was 30. They said, "The Lord told you, 'You will shepherd my people Israel and you will be their ruler.'"

3DF: A shepherd king! And after that, what was your first move as king?

KD: The Jebusites held Jerusalem then, so we snuck in through a secret water shaft. After the victory, we called it the City of David, our capital. The Lord Almighty was blessing me, and the king of Tyre saw it. He even built my palace!

3DF: A royal start! A crown, a capital, and a palace! How did you face your enemies?

KD: The Lord gave us victory! He said, "Go! I am handing the Philistines over to you. Circle behind them and attack by the poplar trees. When you hear the sound of marching in the trees, attack! It means the Lord has gone to strike down the Philistines."

3DF: What was your greatest moment as king?

KD: When we brought the ark of the covenant into Jerusalem! It meant that God was our king, and it became the City of God! I danced right down the street.

3DF: What plans are you making for your kingdom?

KD: Interesting question! I wanted to build a temple for the Lord, but he says my son will. The Lord promises me, "I will make your family line and kingdom last forever."

FLASH-FORWARD >>>

... to the new creation (page 152). An eternal king rules an eternal kingdom. Jesus is the Son of David who defeats sin and death and rules forever.

"Kingdom last forever"

God has huge plans for David's kingdom. A ruler will come from David's family line and rule for ever and ever. He will be the snake crusher promised in Eden (page 17).

★ ★ ★ ★ ★

Why is God's promise important?

And King David's lows

David still makes big mistakes. When he should go to war in spring, he stays in Jerusalem. One night, he looks out of his window and sees a beautiful woman.

3DF: David, your rule then see-sawed. What went wrong?

KD: One, I did not lead the army. Two, I took another man's wife. Three, I plotted murder. I saw a beautiful woman washing on a roof, Bathsheba, the wife of a general, Uriah the Hittite. I slept with her and she became pregnant. Twice I tried to make Uriah sleep with his wife, but he refused while his men were in battle. I sent him to the frontlines where I ordered the men to abandon him… Abandon him to die. *(Sobs)*

3DF: Did anyone know?

KD: I thought I got away with it. I married Bathsheba and she had a son. But the Lord knew. The prophet Nathan told a story: "A rich man with many flocks had a visitor. He prepared a feast for the visitor, but took the only lamb belonging to a poor man and prepared it for the visitor." Nathan's story enraged me! "That man must die!" Nathan replied, "You are the man! The Lord says, 'I made you king, I gave you wives, I gave you all Israel! I would have given you more, but you took Bathsheba, a married woman, and killed her husband, Uriah. Therefore your own sons will die by the sword.'"

3DF: What did God teach you?

KD: I learned to confess my guilt! I said, "I have sinned against the Lord." Our son died a week later. But Bathsheba had a new son and we named him Solomon! The Lord is still good! I wrote a psalm (a song): "Blessed is the one God forgives. When I was silent my bones wasted away, and my strength dried up like in the summer heat. I said, 'I will confess my sin to the Lord,' and he forgave the guilt of my sin."

"Confess my sin"

David learns to say sorry. Unlike Saul, he knows he's done wrong and admits it to God, who forgives his guilt and makes him joyful. Saying sorry changes his life.

★ ★ ★ ★ ★

How does David change after making mistakes?

67

King Solomon's highs

Solomon's kingdom has everything. Before he dies, David told Solomon to obey God. He does, and God blesses Israel more than any nation in history.

INTERVIEW SPECIAL!
POPCORN SALLY MEETS KING SOLOMON

Popcorn Sally: Wise King Solomon! How did you become so wise?

King Solomon: In a dream, the Lord offered me anything. I said, "I don't know how to rule! Give me wisdom to lead and decide what is good." He did! One day, two women brought a problem. One said, "We live in the same house and both of us had sons. One night this woman lay on her baby, killed him, and swapped mine for hers! I found the dead boy, but saw he was not mine!" They argued, so I called for a sword and commanded, "Cut the living child in two and give half to each!" One woman said, "Cut it in two!" The other said, "No, give it to her!" I said, "Here is the real mother!"

PS: You know about a mother's love! And where did your wealth come from?

KS: Also from the Lord! In the same dream he said, "I will give you what you have not asked for." He gave me enormous wealth and promised me long life if I obey him carefully, like my father David. He made us the richest nation in history and our kingdom reaches to the Euphrates, to Philistia, and to Egypt. Everyone has their own vine and fig tree and we have peace on all sides! My people eat and drink and are so happy!

PS: God did promise his blessing! And what's your greatest achievement?

KS: God told David I would build a temple. So I brought cedar wood from Lebanon, which took 30,000 men, and high-grade stone for the foundations, which took 70,000 men. We even had 3,300 men to supervise! It took seven years to build. We put the ark of the covenant inside, which holds the Ten Commandments. It's the sign that God rules the city. The cloud of God's glory fills the Temple – God lives among us!

"Peace on every side"

God fulfils the promises he made to Abraham. Solomon's people are like the stars, his land enjoys peace, and his wealth blesses other nations. The king loves and obeys God!

★ ★ ★ ★ ★

How does God bless Solomon?

The Magnificent Temple

God rules Israel from his Temple. He now has a permanent home on earth among his people. Solomon calls it his magnificent Temple, a place for God to live forever.

SOLOMON'S TEMPLE
Completed 960 or 959 BC

THE MOST HOLY PLACE (9 m cube)

Cloud of God's presence – here God meets his people

Stone prepared at a quarry – no iron tools used at the building site

Two gold cherubim (4.5 m tall with 4.5 m wingspans)

Cedar wood ceiling

THE HOLY PLACE (L 18 m, W 9 m, H 14 m)

Ten golden lampstands

Bronze altar for burnt offerings (L 9 m, W 9 m, W 4.5 m)

The ark of the covenant

Folding doors, covered with gold

Golden altar of incense

Golden table for the bread of the Presence

Folding doors, covered with gold

THE COURTYARD

The "sea" – a metal basin holding 44,000 litres of water, on 12 bronze oxen

"The cloud"
God appears in the Temple as a cloud, as his glory fills the Temple. His presence is so strong that not even the priests can stand!

★ ★ ★ ★ ★

Why is the temple so special?

FLASH-FORWARD >>>

… to Pentecost and the new creation (page 141, 153). Jesus' followers will be a temple where God's Spirit lives, and God will live with his people in heaven for eternity.

And King Solomon's lows!

Sadly, Solomon's heart turns away from God. He has great wisdom and great wealth, but his great many wives turn him away. He ignores God's warnings.

PS: Welcome back for part two! Solomon, tell us about your palace.

KS: Well, that took 13 years to build. I made my treasury, The House of the Forest of Lebanon from cedar, 45 m long. I made the Hall of Pillars, as big as the Temple. Then the Hall of the Throne. Then a palace for me, a palace for my Egyptian wife, of course, and all made from costly stones. The foundations, the great court, inner court…

PS: Stop!! Please, stop! *(Breathes.)* What do others think of this?

KS: Recently the queen of Sheba (Ethiopia) came to test me. When she saw my wisdom, my palace, my food, my sacrifices, she was breathless! She praised God and said, "Blessed be the Lord, who made you a king of justice and goodness."

PS: God blesses the nations through you! Now, tell me about your wives.

KS: Ah yes, my wives. Which ones do you mean? I have Sidonians, Ammonites, Moabites, Edomites, and Hittites…

PS: *(Interrupting)* HOW MANY WIVES DO YOU HAVE?!

KS: Right now…? About 700. And 300 mistresses. But I'm not married to *them*! I'm old now and I love my wives, so I think I should also worship their gods! Like Ashtoreth of the Sidonians and Molek of the Ammonites.

PS: I'm speechless! This is not wise! God warned you not to marry foreign women! They turned away your heart toward other gods. You are not like David! Time to go!

"Heart after other gods"

Solomon's heart is divided. David had a "heart after God", but Solomon cares more about his house than God's, and he ignores Moses' last instructions about marriage.

★ ★ ★ ★ ★

How is Solomon unlike David?

ASK POPCORN SALLY

What kind of king is best?

Most kings say they're best, but good kings say it's not them. No king is perfect, but their people need a good example, and a servant king who puts their people first.

Geography: the divided kingdom

God waits until Solomon dies before dividing his kingdom. A civil war breaks out between the tribes: in the north they make Israel, and in the south they make Judah.

THE DIVIDED KINGDOM

120 years after Saul unites Israel, the kingdoms divide.

ISRAEL

Capital: Samaria

Tribes: Asher, Dan, Gad, Issachar, Ephraim, Manasseh, Naphtali, Reuben, Simeon, Zebulun

King: Jeroboam (one of Solomon's officials)

Jeroboam makes two golden bulls for Israel to worship. Jeroboam: "See, here are the gods that saved you from Egypt."

Bull 1: Bethel   Bull 2: Dan

JUDAH

Capital: Jerusalem

Tribes: Judah and Benjamin

King: Rehoboam (one of Solomon's sons)

Harshly taxes the twelve tribes. Ten tribes rebel and form Israel. Gathers 180,000 men to fight Israel. God stops him.

Judah worships idols and copies other nations.

*Map not to scale

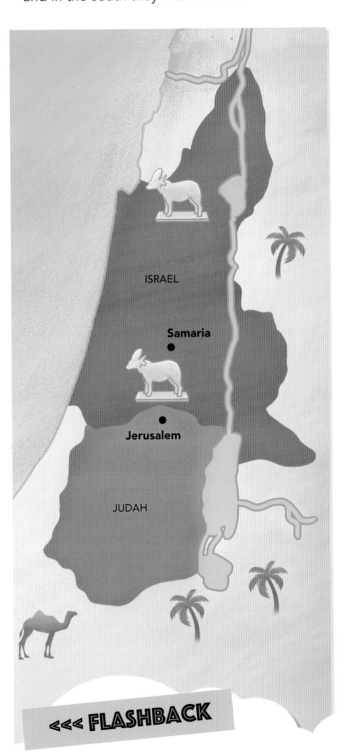

ISRAEL

Samaria •

Jerusalem •

JUDAH

<<< FLASHBACK

... to Aaron (page 45). Jeroboam and Aaron make a golden calf for the people to worship. God hates Jeroboam's sin too.

"Here are the gods"

Jeroboam leads his people astray. He makes Israel gods to stop them visiting Jerusalem's Temple, and even says they rescued Israel from Egypt.

★ ★ ★ ★ ★

How different are Israel and Judah?

ACT 5: PROPHETS AND KINGS

SCENE 1: WARNING AND HOPE!

1 KINGS 17

Elijah and the Widow of Zarephath

Israel's kings get worse. Ahab is their seventh and most evil. He marries the Sidonian princess Jezebel, and leads his people to worship Baal! So God sends a messenger to warn him, the prophet Elijah.

@ZAREPHATH

Elijah

As sure as the God of Israel lives, there will not be dew nor rain over the coming years until I say so.

I have been hiding by the Cherith Brook, east of the Jordan, where the Lord sent ravens to feed me bread and meat! The stream is now dry and the Lord is sending me to Zarephath. He says a widow there will feed me. Zarephath, here I come!

Widow

We've been starving to death. No water for years! I went to gather sticks at the town gates, ready to bake my last morsel of bread and then die with my son. But Elijah turned up and asked for water and my last bit of food! "Fear not, make me a cake and then your flour and oil will not run out!" Now my jar of flour and jug of oil are never empty! The Lord commands it!

Elijah

Your son soon became ill and died. You said, "O man of God, you have shown my sin and caused the death of my son!" I took his body upstairs and cried out to God, "Lord, have you killed her son? Let the child live!" The Lord heard me!

Widow

The Lord raises the dead! "Now I know you are a man of God and the Lord really does speak through you!"

"Live!"

God brings life, not the Canaanite gods. People called Baal the god of rain and Mot the god of death, but only God brings rain and raises the dead.

★ ★ ★ ★ ★

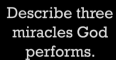

Describe three miracles God performs.

72

The big fight: God vs. Baal

Ahab calls Elijah a troublemaker and blames him for the drought. So Elijah invites him and his 450 prophets of Baal to Mount Carmel. All will see who the real God is.

LIVESTREAM

LIVE @MountCarmel

1min ago FIRE IS FALLING FROM HEAVEN! It's eating up the altar, the wood, the bull, and the soil. It's even swallowed the trench of water! The people are crying, "The Lord is God, he is God!" Now, Elijah is telling them to seize the prophets of Baal.

2mins ago Elijah is calling to his God, "O Lord and God of Abraham, Isaac, and Jacob. Show everyone that you are their God and I am your servant. Answer me, answer me, so that they know your great power."

15mins ago Elijah has dug a trench around his altar and is laying his bull on it. He tells the watchers to pour water all over this sacrifice. Three times! It cannot burn now!

2hrs ago The 450 prophets are waiting for Baal. They're raving around, but no one's answering. This is going on for hours!

4hrs ago It's noon. Elijah is mocking them! "Shout to Baal! He is real! He's just thinking, or going for a poo, or on his travels, or maybe he's asleep!"

8hrs ago The 450 prophets are screaming. "Answer us!" But Baal isn't answering!

9hrs ago Elijah wants to prove who the real God is. "I am the only prophet of God, but Baal has 450. We will make two sacrifices and ask our God and Baal to send fire. He who answers is real." The people agree!

"Answer"

God answers Elijah's prayer straight away. The word "answer" comes up many times. This contest shows God's massive power, and tells the people who to worship.

★ ★ ★ ★ ★

Why does God answer Elijah?

Isaiah comforts King Hezekiah

The Assyrian army destroys Israel in 722 BC. Israel is destroyed. Down in Jerusalem King Hezekiah knows Judah is next, under threat from King Sennacherib. He prays for rescue.

📷 SNAPSCROLL @JERUSALEM

1 SENNACHERIB

Hezekiah, your God lies. He will not save you, just like other gods did not save their nations.

2 SENNACHERIB

Everyday my commander calls you in Hebrew, "Jerusalem, do not listen to Hezekiah! He lies when he says the Lord will rescue you."

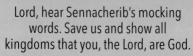

3 HEZEKIAH

Lord, hear Sennacherib's mocking words. Save us and show all kingdoms that you, the Lord, are God.

4 ISAIAH

The Lord says, "Jerusalem laughs at your pride, Sennacherib. Who have you laughed at? At the Lord, the Holy One of Israel."

5 ISAIAH

The Lord says, "The king will not enter or even shoot an arrow. he will return home by the way he came."

6 ISAIAH

The Lord says, "I will defend this city and I will save it for my own sake and David's."

"Jerusalem laughs"

Sennacherib's power does not compare with God's. Both sides mock each other, but God has the last word. He humbles proud Sennacherib and saves his people.

★ ★ ★ ★ ★

How does God answer Hezekiah?

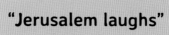

7 HEZEKIAH

What a sight this morning. 185,000 soldiers of Sennacherib's army lie dead. The Lord has sent his angel. We're saved!

8 HEZEKIAH

Sennacherib is going home! Something tells me his people won't be happy.

Isaiah sees the future

Hezekiah soon becomes proud before God. Messengers come from powerful Babylon, and Hezekiah shows them his treasures. Isaiah explains God's punishment.

 eMessenger

From: Isaiah, the Lord's prophet

To: King Hezekiah

Subject: You fool! Babylon will return!

Dear Hezekiah, thirteenth king of Judah,

I am writing the words of the Lord Almighty. The king of Babylon sent messengers and gifts to you because he heard you were ill. But you showed them your stores, your silver, gold, spices, fine olive oil, your entire armoury, and all your treasures! There's nothing you did not show them in your palace or in all your kingdom!

Hear the Lord Almighty, "One day, Babylon will take everything in your palace and everything the kings before you have stored up. They will leave nothing behind! Your children will serve in the palace of Babylon, unable to have their own children."

Hezekiah, you only think of yourself! You say, "the word of the Lord is good" because you expect only peace and safety in your lifetime.

But remember my old message of hope. "Some of God's people will return to Jerusalem, to the Mighty God. Your people are like the sand by the sea, but only a small remnant will return."

<<< FLASHBACK

... to Moses' warnings (page 51). God promised that disobedience leads to exile. Exile means living away from God and his Temple. Adam and Eve were also exiled for sin.

"Take everything"

God brings warnings and hope. Babylon will destroy Judah and take its people into exile. Only some will return. Hezekiah acts like he doesn't care, just like his people.

★ ★ ★ ★ ★

Why should Judah listen to God?

Jeremiah and the clay jar

God warns Judah with another prophet, Jeremiah. Destruction is coming! No one listens to persistent Jeremiah, so God sends him to a pottery to use some visual aids…

 eMessenger

From: Jeremiah, the Lord's prophet

To: Jerusalem-ALL

Subject: Destruction is coming! DON'T IGNORE!

Hear the Lord Almighty. "Listen! I am bringing a disaster that will make your ears tingle! You have abandoned me! You worshipped foreign gods and burned incense to them in the temples. They are gods you and your fathers have not known! And you even burned your children as sacrifices to the false god Baal!

"Soon people will call this place the Valley of Slaughter. Your people will die by the sword, and birds and beasts will eat your bodies. All who pass will be appalled at the devastation. Jerusalem will be under siege and your people will even eat each other!"

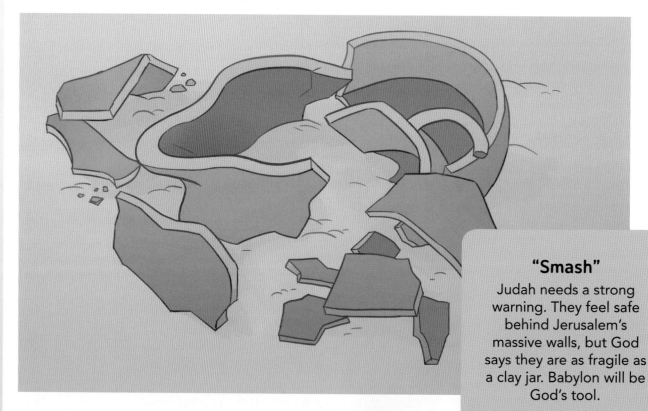

The Lord says, "See this clay jar! I will bring another nation to smash Judah and Jerusalem like this jar. I will smash your nation so it cannot be repaired. Judah will be a barren wasteland and you will serve the king of Babylon for 70 years."

"Smash"
Judah needs a strong warning. They feel safe behind Jerusalem's massive walls, but God says they are as fragile as a clay jar. Babylon will be God's tool.

★ ★ ★ ★ ★

What does the clay jar teach Judah?

Everyone ignores Jeremiah

In 597 BC, Nebuchadnezzar destroys Judah and exiles many, including the prophet Ezekiel. The people of Jerusalem rebel and the Babylonians return in 586 BC. Persistent Jeremiah warns the king.

 PHOTOS

 FRIENDS

 EVENTS

@JERUSALEM

Jeremiah

King Zedekiah! Egypt has protected us until now, but they are leaving and Babylon will return to burn down our city!

Sentry Irijah

Traitor! I just found Jeremiah abandoning our city! He says he was visiting his hometown. Lies! We have beaten him and put him in prison!

Zedekiah

Jeremiah, you asked me to release you and I did. I asked you for good news, and what came? TERRIBLE NEWS! The king of Babylon will not take me! My officials say you are harming our people and must die. I place you in their hands!

Ebed-Melek

My lord the king, I am one of your servants. These men have done evil and put Jeremiah in a dry water cistern. He now lies in mud starving to death.

Zedekiah

No! Take 30 men and lift Jeremiah out of the cistern before he dies.

Jeremiah

I'm alive! 30 men used worn-out clothes to lift me from the pit. Zedekiah, you must surrender! If not, the king of Babylon will burn this city and you will not escape.

"Surrender!"

The people of Judah and Zedekiah are proud. They ignore God, hate his warnings, and try to kill his prophet. Soon the Babylonians smash Jerusalem, imprison and blind Zedekiah, and exile his people.

★ ★ ★ ★ ★

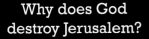

Why does God destroy Jerusalem?

ASK POPCORN SALLY

Aren't the prophets only doom and gloom?

Often, but not only! God warns his people, but he also gives hope. Jeremiah says God has plans to prosper and not harm his people, plans to give hope and a future.

Ezekiel's street theatre

Ezekiel is God's prophet in Babylon. In 593 BC he warns the exiles there about the coming destruction on Jerusalem, but they ignore him. God tells Ezekiel to do some acting!

📷 SNAPSCROLL @BABYLON

1 EZEKIEL

This brick represents Jerusalem. The city is surrounded, under siege.

2 EZEKIEL

I am acting out God's part. The Lord is rejecting the city. This iron pan stands as an iron wall between him and Jerusalem.

3 EZEKIEL

Selfie! I will lie on my left for 390 days! One day for each year of punishment for Israel.

4 EZEKIEL

Me again! I will now lie on my right another 40 days! One day for each year of punishment for Judah!

5 EZEKIEL

The Lord will cut off the food supply to Jerusalem. See my food rations: a tiny bit of bread and two cups of water.

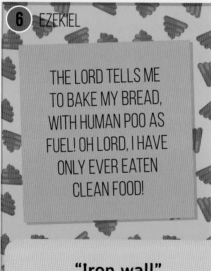

6 EZEKIEL

THE LORD TELLS ME TO BAKE MY BREAD, WITH HUMAN POO AS FUEL! OH LORD, I HAVE ONLY EVER EATEN CLEAN FOOD!

7 EZEKIEL

PHEW! THE LORD SAYS I CAN BAKE MY BREAD OVER COW'S DUNG. BETTER!

8 EZEKIEL

The Lord will cut off our food supply! In misery we will eat rationed food and drink rationed water. We will starve here.

"Iron wall"

God rejects Jerusalem. The iron pan cuts them off from God. He can help, but he will not. Jerusalem must listen to God's warnings because he will punish them.

★ ★ ★ ★ ★

What does Ezekiel's performance mean?

Ezekiel's hope for the exiles

The exiles have lost all hope. Babylon destroys Jerusalem and its Temple in 586 BC, but God has a message of hope for them and he shows it to Ezekiel…

 eMessenger

From: Ezekiel, the Lord's prophet in Babylon

To: Exiles-ALL

Subject: HOPE! You want to read this!

The Lord says, "I will bring you back home! I will remove your heart of stone and give you a heart of flesh! Then you will be my people and I will be your God."

He has shown me a vision of a valley full of dry bones. He has a message for them: "Hear the Lord! I will breathe life into you and you will live. I will put muscle, flesh, and skin on you. You will live and know that I am the Lord."

I, Ezekiel, spoke to the bones and a rattling began. The bones joined, bone to bone. Muscle, flesh and skin covered them. But they had no breath. The Lord said, "Tell the breath: 'Come from the four winds and breathe life on these dead.'" I spoke and the bones came to life and became an extremely large army. We say, "Our bones are dried up and our hope is gone: God has cut us off." But listen! The Lord will raise us to life and return us to Israel! He will put his Spirit in us and we will live again!

"Heart of flesh"

God gives hope. He will bring his people back home and give them a heart transplant. One day, his Spirit will give them a heart that wants to obey him.

★ ★ ★ ★ ★

FLASH-FORWARD >>>

… to Pentecost (page 141). God's Spirit will give his people a new heart, one that loves to obey him. The Holy Spirit will give new life.

Why should the exiles have hope?

Daniel's diet

Daniel is one of the exiles in Babylon, and he faces a test of faith. King Nebuchadnezzar, king of Babylon, wants Daniel to learn his ways to serve in his court.

 PHOTOS

 FRIENDS

 EVENTS

@BABYLON

Chief servant

I will teach you for three years, then you will meet the king. Now you need Babylonian names. I give Daniel the name Belteshazzar. As for your friends, they will be Shadrach, Meshach, and Abednego.

Daniel

Oh, chief servant, we will not dirty ourselves with the king's food. Allow us only to eat vegetables and drink water for ten days. Do not fear the king, who chose our food and drink. We will not look worse than the men who eat his food.

"Test us"

Daniel is stubbornly confident in God. He is tested, and he makes the servant test God. The servant sees how only God gives wisdom and strength, not the food.

★ ★ ★ ★ ★

How does Daniel pass his test of faith?

Chief servant

That's impossible! After ten days, you are finer and far healthier than all the others! From now on, I'm giving you vegetables and water!

Daniel

God has given me, Shadrach, Meshach, and Abednego skill in all kinds of writing and wisdom. He even helps me understand all kinds of visions and dreams!

Nebuchadnezzar

Amazing! I have talked with these men and I find no equal to them. They will now enter my service. In fact, I have found them ten times wiser than all the magicians in all my vast kingdom. Well done!

Death by fiery furnace

Nebuchadnezzar likes to show off his power. One day he builds a golden statue, which everyone must worship when music is played, or face death! The Jews refuse.

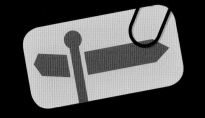

LIVESTREAM

LIVE @Babylon

now	What's this? Nebuchadnezzar PROMOTES Shadrach, Meshach, and Abednego and forbids anyone accusing them of anything? Or they will be torn limb from limb?! Neb says no other god can rescue like this!
2mins ago	Neb is calling them out of the fire! "You three, servants of the Most High God, come out and come here!" They aren't hurt! Not even a hair on their head is burned! They don't even *smell* of fire!
5mins ago	Neb is amazed. "I see four men in the fire, not tied up. They're walking around and aren't hurt! The fourth man is like a son of the gods."
20mins ago	The king is furious! He has ordered the fire to be superheated, seven times hotter than usual! Soldiers are tying up Shadrach, Meshach, and Abednego and throwing them in. Wait! The fire has even killed the soldiers!
2hrs ago	Big mistake. The men say, "Our God can save us from the fire and from you, O King. Even if he doesn't, we will not worship that statue."
2hrs 2mins ago	Neb is furious! "Is it true you won't serve my gods or worship my statue? I will throw you into a fiery furnace! Who is this god anyway?"
2hrs 10mins ago	Breaking News! We hear that certain Jews will not bow down to Neb's statue! And even more, they're important people in Babylon!

"Seven times hotter"

The king wants to show off his power. But in the end his order kills his own strong soldiers, and God's power saves the three exiles. Neb begins to see who the Most High is.

★ ★ ★ ★ ★

How is this story about power?

81

Bad news for Belshazzar

Nebuchadnezzar's son also needs a lesson about power. He invites 1000 lords to a feast and uses the goblets taken from Jerusalem's Temple. He's mocking God.

▶ LIVESTREAM

ממתוס
ננקפי
אא לרן

LIVE @Babylon

1min ago	THE KING IS DEAD!! The Medes have conquered Babylon. Long live Darius the Mede, our new king!
2hrs ago	Praise Belshazzar the Noble! He rewards Daniel anyway! See his purple clothes and gold chain.
2hrs ago	Daniel interprets! "MENE, MENE, TEKEL, PARSIN. God has numbered your days and is dividing your kingdom between Medes and Persians."
2hrs ago	Daniel replies, "Keep your gifts, O King. The Most High gave your father great power, but also took it away. You knew this, but you did not humble yourself. You have lifted yourself up against the Lord of heaven and mocked him."
2hrs ago	Bel is desperate! He's begging Daniel! "I hear the spirit of the gods is in you. Explain to me the writing on the wall! I will clothe you in purple, give you a gold chain, and make you third in my kingdom!"
3hrs ago	What's this? The fingers of a human hand are writing on the wall. We can all see it. The king is terrified, white as a sheet, and can barely stand! He's calling his wise men. Help! Hold on – our queen speaks: "O King, live forever! I know a man, chief among enchanters. Daniel."
3hrs ago	Happy times! Belshazzar begins with a toast. We're drinking from the goblets of Jerusalem, and praising the gods of gold, silver, and bronze.

"Numbered your days"

Belshazzar discovers that mocking God is a mistake. He and the queen expect to live for ages, but the Most High ends his life that night. The reign of Babylon is over.

What are Belshazzar's mistakes?

Death by hungry lions

Daniel needs another rescue. Rulers in Babylon have made a rule that only the new king Darius the Mede may be worshipped. Or face death by hungry lions!

 SNAPSCROLL @BABYLON

1 RULERS

Daniel does not worship the king! Here is proof! We must tell the king Daniel is praying to his God three times a day. Just like before!

2 RULERS

O King, Daniel is an exile from Judah and ignores you and your order! He still prays three times every day, just like before!

3 DARIUS

Allow me to think. How can I rescue Daniel now?

4 RULERS

O King, now it is night! Remember that, in the laws of the Medes and Persians, no order you make can be changed! Daniel must die!

5 DARIUS

O Daniel, may your God rescue you!

6 DARIUS

I prayed but couldn't sleep all night. Daniel, has your God saved you?

7 DANIEL

O King, live forever! My God sent an angel to shut the lions' mouths. I am blameless before him and before you.

8 DARIUS

Let these men who hated Daniel and their families die! May people fear the God of Daniel, who lives and rules forever.

"Daniel"

Only God judges Daniel's fate and not the rulers, who think they are in charge. Daniel means "God is my judge". The rulers make laws to force Darius to kill him, but Daniel is blameless.

★ ★ ★ ★ ★

How and why does God save Daniel?

Ezra teaches the Law

God's people need a teacher. After 70 years, Persian kings take over and send the Jews home. Ezra is the perfect man to help them. He's serious about God's Law!

 **PHOTOS**

 **FRIENDS**

 **EVENTS**

@JERUSALEM

King Artaxerxes

Ezra, you are skilled in the Law of your God. Now return to Jerusalem, with anyone who wants to go, and take silver and gold for your God's Temple. Choose men to judge and lead the people; men who also know your God's laws.

Ezra

Hello, Jerusalem! I'm tired after a four-month journey but keen to teach God's Law!

City rulers

The people and priests and Levites have married foreigners. Now our holy, separate nation is mixed with just about everyone.

Ezra

I'm appalled, ashamed at our sin. I tear my clothes and pull my hair. Lord, we have broken your laws and soon our children will worship foreign gods too.

Sons of Elam

We're crying bitterly. We all broke God's laws. Let's make an oath: we will send away these foreign wives and children. We must turn God's anger away!

Ezra

Men and women! All who are old enough to understand assemble at daybreak. Day after day, I will read out God's Law. Listen and understand! The Levites will walk among you and teach you.

"Understand"

Israel repeats past mistakes. They must understand that God made them different, to live differently. They take their sin seriously and obey God's Law again.

★ ★ ★ ★ ★

Why must the people understand God's Law?

Nehemiah rebuilds the walls

Jerusalem has no protection. Their walls and gates are ruined. In Persia, King Artaxerxes sends his cupbearer Nehemiah home to lead the work. But he has enemies.

📷 SNAPSCROLL @JERUSALEM

1 NEHEMIAH

Inspection time! I've seen the Jackal Well, the Dung Gate, and the city walls… But my horse could not pass the Fountain Gate and King's Pool.

2 NEHEMIAH

We're in trouble! Let's rebuild the walls so we are no longer disgraced.

3 RULERS

We're agreed! Let everyone build the section near to their home.

4 TOBIAH THE AMMONITE

HAH! EVEN A FOX COULD KNOCK IT OVER!

5 NEHEMIAH

FIRST THEY MOCK US, AND NOW THEY SPREAD GOSSIP. LET HALF OF US STAND GUARD! REMEMBER THE LORD, GREAT AND AWESOME, AND FIGHT FOR YOUR PEOPLE AND HOMES! DO NOT FEAR THEM! REMEMBER THE LORD, WHO IS GREAT AND AWESOME, AND FIGHT FOR YOUR FAMILIES AND HOMES.

6 SANBALLAT THE HORONITE

Nehemiah, talk to me and Tobiah on neutral ground! Come! This is the fifth time of asking. Stop saying you must finish the job!

7 NEHEMIAH

SANBALLAT, YOUR LETTER CLAIMS WE NEED OUR WALLS BECAUSE WE PLAN TO REVOLT. YOU EVEN CLAIM I WANT TO BE KING! YOU INVENT STORIES IN YOUR HEAD!

8 NEHEMIAH

Job done! Our enemies can see how God helped us. Now let Ezra teach God's Law!

"Remember… and fight"

Nehemiah is a resilient man. His enemies use four tactics to stop his work, but the Jews work hard and finish the walls in 52 days. Nehemiah remembers God throughout.

★ ★ ★ ★ ★

Why is Nehemiah successful?

Esther becomes queen of Persia

Back in Persia, King Xerxes rules all people from Ethiopia to India. Soon the Jews face total destruction, and Xerxes' new queen looks like the only person who can save them.

CITY CHAT

@SUSA

 **PHOTOS**

 **FRIENDS**

EVENTS

Xerxes

I have a new queen: Esther! My old queen, Vashti, refused to obey me!

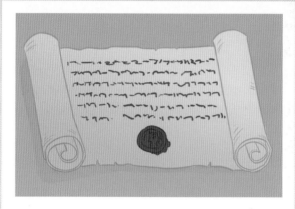

Esther

My lord the king, there is a conspiracy to kill you! A Jewish man called Mordecai overheard their plot and has told me to tell you.

Xerxes

These men shall be HANGED! Mordecai has saved me.

Haman

I am the prime minister and Xerxes commands all to bow to me! Even you, Mordecai! Every day you refuse and I am furious! Because of you, I will kill all the Jews in the Persian Empire. Hear my orders! On the 13th day of the 12th month, I order every Jew in the king's empire to be killed – young and old, women and children. This is sealed with the king's ring.

Mordecai

Esther, my cousin, all the Jews are crying bitterly! You are Jewish too and must tell Xerxes. Plead with him for your people!

Esther

But if anyone sees the king without being called, they will die! I haven't been called for 30 days!

Mordecai

You will not escape death either! If you stay silent, rescue will come from another place. Maybe you became queen for such a time as this!

Esther

Pray for me with every Jew in Susa. In three days, I will see the king. If I die, I die.

"Rescue will come"

God works in the background. Although no one says his name, God helps Esther and her cousin Mordecai, and they know he will rescue his people.

★ ★ ★ ★ ★

What plans do Haman and Mordecai make?

Esther's clever banquets

God brings a hilarious rescue. Esther goes to see Xerxes and he offers her anything, up to half his kingdom! So she invites him to a banquet with Haman.

LIVESTREAM

LIVE @Susa

0mins ago What a reversal! The king has hanged Haman on his own gallows! Hahaha! Generous King Xerxes! Queen Esther has Haman's home and Mordecai is prime minister! The Jews are saved!

9mins ago Xerxes is raging at Haman and has gone out to think. What's this? Haman is on Esther's seat begging for his life. The king's back! "Will he even attack my queen in my own home?" Men are grabbing Haman, and a servant has mentioned his gallows for Mordecai!

12mins ago It's Esther's second feast. Haman seems unhappy tonight. It's about to get worse! The king is asking Esther, "Request anything, up to half my kingdom!" She says she's a Jew, but her people will soon be killed. Xerxes is asking who has dared to do this. Vile Haman! Uh oh.

9hrs ago Hilarious! Xerxes has praised Mordecai, and Haman has to dress Mordecai in royal robes and put him on the royal horse! Haman wanted this for himself! He never expected this! Look how angry he is!

12hrs ago The king can't sleep. He has just heard that he never praised Mordecai for saving his life. He sure will now. But Haman has arrived to discuss hanging Mordecai on gallows he has built! Xerxes asks him how he should treat the man he delights to praise. Haman thinks it's him – he's listing loads of things!

24hrs ago Esther did not ask her question at her banquet – she's making Xerxes wait until tomorrow. But Haman's showing off how the king and queen love to praise him. He will get what he deserves.

"Praise"

Haman is competing with Mordecai for praise. But he doesn't realize that God is on Mordecai's side! Xerxes rewards loyalty, and Haman gets justice.

★ ★ ★ ★ ★

Why is Haman doomed?

Jonah runs from God

The prophet Jonah has lots to learn. He desperately tries to disobey God, and what happens is really funny. He tries his best to control the situation, but God is clearly the one in control.

📷 SNAPSCROLL @JOPPAPORT

1 JONAH

Me, go to Nineveh? Tell them how wicked they are? NO WAY! This boat is for Tarshish – perfect! I'm running from God!

2 SAILORS

Help! Some god has hurled this storm on us! Everyone pray and toss out the cargo! Hurl it and quick!

3 CAPTAIN

Whaaat!? You're sleeping when we're going to die?! You're the prophet and we're the ones praying! PRAY! Maybe your god will save us.

4 SAILORS

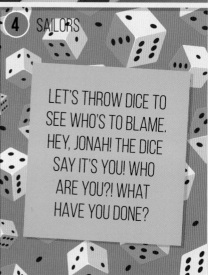

LET'S THROW DICE TO SEE WHO'S TO BLAME. HEY, JONAH! THE DICE SAY IT'S YOU! WHO ARE YOU?! WHAT HAVE YOU DONE?

5 JONAH

I am a Hebrew. I respect the Lord, the God of heaven, who made the sea and dry land, but I am running away from him. The sea will die down if you hurl me in.

6 SAILORS

Let's hurl him in. O Lord, do not punish us for Jonah's life! We will fear and worship you.

7 JONAH

The storm is stopping…! Hang on, that's a big fish! This. Is. It!

8 JONAH

LORD, I CRIED TO YOU AND YOU HEARD ME FROM THE FISH'S BELLY. I HAVE REMEMBERED YOU, THE GOD WHO SAVES!

"Made sea and dry land"

Jonah's plan is a disaster! He runs, but God made the sea. He sleeps, but the sailors pray. He hides, but the dice reveal him. He expects to die, but a big fish swallows and takes him.

★ ★ ★ ★ ★

What does Jonah need to learn?

Jonah speaks against Nineveh

Jonah's bad moods are also funny. The big fish takes him to land and God sends him to Nineveh again. 120,000 people live there, and their response really annoys him.

 **PHOTOS**

 **FRIENDS**

 **EVENTS**

@NINEVEH

Jonah

In 40 days, Nineveh will be destroyed!

King of Nineveh

All our people believe God, from the greatest to the least! We believe and really do mourn our sin.

King of Nineveh

Nineveh, hear my order! All must wear sackcloth and call to God. Turn from evil! God may turn from his anger and we may live!

Jonah

O Lord, I said this would happen! That's why I went to Tarshish!
I knew you are compassionate, slow to anger, completely loving, and would stop from sending disaster. Now kill me! I want to die! AGGHHH!!!

Jonah

Sitting to the east of the city now. Just waiting to see what might happen. Loving the shade of this plant here.

Jonah

WHYYYY??!!! Yesterday I had a vine, but a worm has eaten it! And this scorching east wind is too much. I'M SO ANGRY I WANT TO DIE!

Jonah

The Lord says I care for the plant, but I did not make it grow. He says, "Should I not then care for great Nineveh and its 120,000 people who cannot tell their right from their left?"

"Compassion"

Moody Jonah never learns! He can't believe Nineveh's good reaction to God, and is angrier about a dead vine than a saved city! He should love God's compassion!

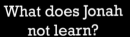

What does Jonah not learn?

Geography: prophets and kings

Kingdoms come and go, but God's message stays the same.
God's prophets always bring warning and hope to his rebellious people.

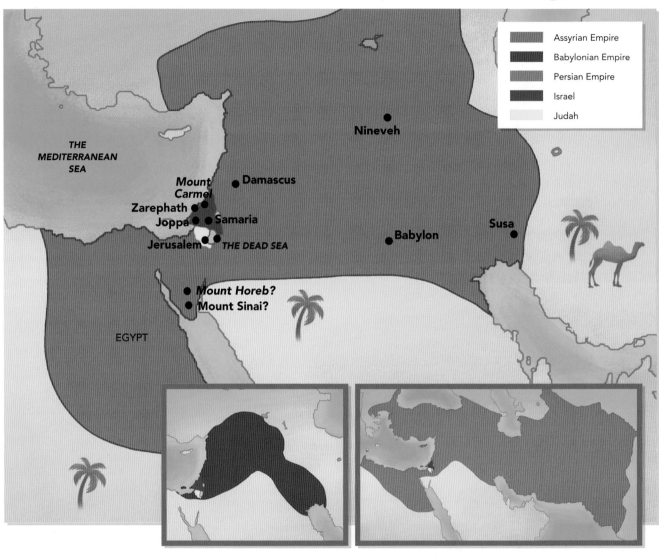

- **Israel,** the northern kingdom, is destroyed in 722 BC by an Assyrian army.

- **Samaria** is Israel's capital. After the Assyrians defeat them, the Samaritans marry their enemy and have children with them.

- **Judah**, the southern kingdom, is attacked many times by Assyria and Babylonia.

- **Jerusalem,** Judah's capital, was beaten in 597 BC and 586 BC and its people exiled.

- **Mount Carmel** was where Elijah faced the 450 prophets of Baal.

- **Zarephath** was home to the widow Elijah met.

- **The Assyrian empire** was led by Sennacherib against Hezekiah.

- **The Babylonian empire** was led by Nebuchadnezzar and Belshazzar.

- **Babylon,** the Babylonian capital, was home to Ezekiel and Daniel.

- **The Persian empire** was led by Cyrus, Darius, Artaxerxes, and Xerxes.

- **Susa** was a royal city in Persia and was home to Esther and Xerxes.

- **Joppa** was where Jonah boarded a boat for Tarshish (in Spain).

- **Nineveh** (in Iraq) had 120,000 people and took three days to cross. Jonah came here.

- **Mount Horeb (probably Mount Sinai)**, where Elijah ran to after beating the prophets of Baal.

*Maps not to scale

Timeline: prophets and kings

A rocky 500 years of kings pass. God's people live under good kings and bad, Jewish and foreign. They still await God's promised king who will rule forever.

Kingdom divides into Israel and Judah.	Elijah serves Israel for 25 years.	Jonah serves Israel.	Isaiah serves Judah for 40 years.	Fall of Samaria (Israel).
931 BC	**875**	**760**	**740**	**722**

Nebuchadnezzar takes more exiles to Babylon, including Ezekiel.	Nebuchadnezzar takes exiles to Babylon, with Daniel, who serves 69 years.	Jeremiah speaks to Judah for 40 years.	Sennacherib attacks Jerusalem and loses. 185,000 Assyrians die.
597	**605**	**627**	**701**

Ezekiel speaks to the exiles in Babylon for 22 years.	Nebuchadnezzar destroys Jerusalem completely, taking many more exiles.	Cyrus of Persia conquers Babylon.	1st return of exiles to Jerusalem.	Temple rebuilding begins.
593	**586**	**539**	**538**	**536**

3rd return of exiles with Nehemiah, in Artaxerxes' 20th year.	2nd return of exiles with Ezra, in Artaxerxes' 7th year.	Esther becomes queen of Persia.	Temple is completed.
445	**458**	**478**	**516**

ASK POPCORN SALLY

Which prophet do you like the most?

I enjoy them all! I love Elijah's miracles, Isaiah's calmness, Jeremiah's persistence, Ezekiel's hope, Daniel's faithfulness, and Jonah's moodiness!

FLASH-FORWARD >>>

... to Jesus' birth (page 100). BC means "Before Christ". These dates lead up to Jesus' birth. He will be a prophet to teach the people, a priest to offer a sacrifice, and a king to rule them.

SCENE 2: GLIMPSES OF THE MESSIAH

A Son of Eve, Abraham, and David

Since the Fall, God has been promising a Messiah, a Chosen One. The Chosen One will save, bless, and rule God's people. His people can see him from afar.

"SNAKE, ONE OF THE WOMAN'S DESCENDANTS WILL CRUSH YOUR HEAD, BUT YOU WILL STRIKE HER HEEL."

Genesis 3:15

FLASH-FORWARD >>>

… to the Cross (page 132). A snake crusher will defeat the devil and pay for sin by dying.

"ABRAHAM, I WILL BLESS ALL THE NATIONS ON EARTH THROUGH YOU."

Genesis 12:3

FLASH-FORWARD >>>

… to the new creation (page 152). A Son of Abraham will bless the world and people will praise God.

"Will"

God is serious about his promises. He sees what the world needs and he gives a Messiah to save his people from sin, to bless all the world, and to rule for eternity.

★ ★ ★ ★ ★

How will God fulfil his promises?

"I WILL BE HIS FATHER AND HE WILL BE MY SON. I WILL MAKE YOUR FAMILY LINE AND KINGDOM LAST FOREVER."

2 Samuel 7:14, 16

FLASH-FORWARD >>>

… to the new creation (page 152). A Son of David will rule for eternity, the Son of the Father – the Son of God.

The Messiah's birth

The Chosen One will have a special birth. God wants his people to spot exactly who the Messiah is, and to worship him. They must not mistake who he is.

"A VIRGIN WILL BECOME PREGNANT! SHE WILL HAVE A SON AND CALL HIM IMMANUEL – 'GOD IS WITH US'."

Isaiah 7:14

FLASH-FORWARD >>>

… to Mary (page 99). A virgin woman who has never slept with a man will give birth to Emmanuel, God with us.

"A CHILD IS BORN, CALLED WONDERFUL COUNSELLOR, MIGHTY GOD, EVERLASTING FATHER, PRINCE OF PEACE."

Isaiah 9:6

FLASH-FORWARD >>>

… to the shepherds and angels (page 100). A boy who is God himself will bring peace to many people.

"BETHLEHEM! O SMALL VILLAGE! A RULER WILL COME FROM YOU, FROM THE DISTANT PAST."

Micah 5:2

FLASH-FORWARD >>>

… to Bethlehem (page 101). A small village, David's hometown, will produce a ruler who is descended from Abraham and David.

"Ruler"

The baby will get a lot of attention. His mother will be a virgin, making him a miracle baby. He will be God himself. And he will be a ruler, even from birth.

★ ★ ★ ★ ★

How will God fulfil his promises?

The servant Messiah

God's ruler will surprise everyone. God's Messiah, his Chosen One, will be glorious *and* humble! He promises a Messiah who will serve and die for his people.

"REJOICE, JERUSALEM! YOUR KING IS COMING! HE RIDES LOWLY AND VICTORIOUS ON A YOUNG DONKEY, A COLT."

Zechariah 9:9

FLASH-FORWARD >>>

... to Jesus entering Jerusalem (page 128). The king will ride on a donkey, not a glorious horse of war.

"THEY WILL DIVIDE MY CLOTHES AMONG THEM AND CAST LOTS FOR THEM."

Psalm 22:18

FLASH-FORWARD >>>

... to the soldiers at the Cross (page 132). People will gamble for the king's clothes, his last possessions.

"Rejoice"

The people must celebrate the death of their king! God plans for the Messiah to die, because his death will crush the snake (defeat the devil) and pay for sin.

How will this king surprise people?

"THE CHOSEN ONE WILL DIE WITHOUT A SINGLE POSSESSION."

Daniel 9:26

FLASH-FORWARD >>>

... to the Cross (page 133). The Chosen One will die alone.

The Messiah will pay for sins

This king will conquer sin. Most kings conquer countries, but the Messiah sees his people's biggest problem. He will rescue them from sin by dying in their place.

THE SUFFERING SERVANT

"WHO WILL BELIEVE THE SERVANT? HE HAS NO BEAUTY OR MAJESTY TO DRAW US TO HIM. MEN DESPISED AND REJECTED HIM, AND HE WAS A MAN OF SORROWS. WE LOOKED AWAY FROM HIM AND DID NOT ADMIRE HIM.

"HE CARRIED OUR SUFFERINGS! WE THOUGHT GOD PUNISHED HIM FOR HIS OWN SINS, BUT HE WAS PIERCED FOR OUR REBELLION AND CRUSHED FOR OUR SINS! HIS SUFFERINGS BROUGHT US PEACE, AND HIS WOUNDS HAVE HEALED US.

"WE ALL, LIKE SHEEP, HAVE GONE ASTRAY. ALL OF US TURNED TO OUR OWN WAY, AND THE LORD LAID ON HIM THE SIN OF US ALL."

Isaiah 53:1–6

FLASH-FORWARD >>>

... to the Cross (page 133). The Chosen One will suffer God's anger against sin.

ASK 3D FREDDIE

Are these really about Jesus?

What do you think? For over 300 years, the prophets describe a man who must fulfil every promise, even the one about where he is born. And Jesus matches them all!

"He was"

The Chosen One rescues people across history. Isaiah talks about the Messiah in the past tense because it is certain. Sometimes people speak about the future as if it has already happened.

★ ★ ★ ★ ★

Why will the Messiah die?

INTERMISSION: THE STORY SO FAR

Old Testament: check! That's the fastest 2,000 years I've ever known. Phew!

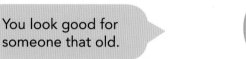

You look good for someone that old.

Yes, yes, good joke. It's just… well, time for a catch-up. What's happened so far? What should I know if I dozed off for a few minutes?!

The Old Testament is a story about God and his people. He created them important, to live with him. But they turned their backs on him and their sin grew worse and worse. Sin and death spread and the problem looked impossible to fix.

So God steps in with some promises, or covenants! He chose Abraham and blessed his family with many children, until his people became slaves in Egypt. God used Moses to rescue his people, bless them, and give them their very own land, Canaan.

But the Israelite nation acted just like foreign nations and worshipped foreign gods. God gave them judges like Gideon and Samson to save them from their enemies, until they wanted kings to be like the countries around them.

History! I love it! We learn so much. But Israel didn't learn. They forgot that God made them different, and also forgot to *be* different. King David understood, but most kings rejected God. So God sent prophets.

The prophets warned about future destruction – turn to God or be destroyed. But they also gave hope. God promised to bring his people home from exile, and bring a Messiah, a Chosen One. He's a king who fixes the problem of sin once and for all.

Bingo! So now we're waiting… Who's the Messiah, and how will we recognize him?

THE NEW TESTAMENT

ACT 6: THE PROMISED KING

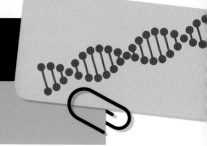

SCENE 1: THE SON OF...

The Wait is Over!

Fast forward 400 years: a man is born who fits the description for the Messiah. "Christ" is the Greek word for the Chosen One. The people recognize his nametag.

FAMILY TREE OF THE PROMISED KING

Jesus the Christ

Joseph + Mary

(many generations)

Hezekiah

(many generations)

Rehoboam

Solomon

David + Bathsheba

Jesse

Obed

Boaz + Ruth

Salmon + Rahab

(many generations)

Judah

Jacob + Leah

Isaac + Rebekah

Abraham + Sarah

(many generations)

Adam + Eve

"The Son of Abraham and David"

The family tree creates excitement. As Son (descendant) of Abraham, Jesus will bless the whole world. As the Son of David, he is the promised king to rule for eternity.

★ ★ ★ ★ ★

What will the Chosen One do?

ASK 3D FREDDIE

Did Jesus have four fathers?

Funny! No, "son" means descendant, so Jesus descends from Joseph, David, Abraham, and God. Jesus' real Father is God, which we will see next.

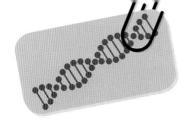

The Wait is Over!

Jesus has a surprising father. In Nazareth, Mary and Joseph are getting married. But before that, Mary becomes pregnant and Joseph is not the father! Who is?

ROMAN CENSUS REPORT

By order of Emperor Augustus   Counting the Roman Empire, 6 BC

Location: *Bethlehem in Judea*

To register: *Joseph, Mary, and Jesus*

Special report: *Joseph claims he is not the father. They say the baby is God's.*

Mary says an angel called Gabriel spoke to her in Nazareth: "God is with you! You will have a son and call him Jesus, who will be great and the Son of the Most High. One day, he will have David's throne and his kingdom will last for eternity." Mary says she is still a virgin, but an angel told her who the father was. "The Spirit of the Most High will make you pregnant. Therefore, the boy will be holy and will be called the Son of God." Mary says she accepts this.

Joseph reports he planned to break the engagement with Mary, but then he met the angel. "Joseph, Son of David, do not be afraid to marry Mary. Her son is from the Holy Spirit. You will call him Jesus, because he will save his people from their sins."

They say their prophet Isaiah said, "a virgin will give birth to a son, Immanuel" (meaning "God is with us").

Note: *Joseph's hometown is Bethlehem and he is from David's family line, so Mary and Joseph had to go there to register for the census.*

 **<<< FLASHBACK**

… to David (page 66). Gabriel reminds Mary how a king from David's family line will rule for eternity. The Christ must be born in Bethlehem.

"Son of God"

Jesus is God himself. Gabriel says his Father is the Most High, and Mary will be pregnant through the Holy Spirit.

★ ★ ★ ★ ★

Explain three titles for Mary's son.

99

Shepherds visit Jesus

An angel announces the birth first. Mary and Joseph have not found a guest room for Mary to give birth. Once he is born they lay Jesus in a manger (a feeding trough). Soon visitors arrive...

BEHIND THE SCENES WITH THE SHEPHERDS!

Script: Finding the King

ANGEL

(God's glory shines around shepherds. Shepherds are terrified.)

Do not fear! I have good news! Today in David's town a saviour is born. He is the Christ, the Lord. Find the baby lying in a manger.

ARMY OF ANGELS

(Suddenly appear.)

Glory to God in the highest heaven, and peace to his people.

(Angel and army of angels disappear.)

SHEPHERDS

Let's go to Bethlehem!

(See Jesus in the feeding trough.)

(Leave praising and glorifying God. Tell others they meet.)

◀◀◀ FLASHBACK

... to Isaiah (page 93). The angels say Jesus will bring peace. Isaiah called the Messiah "mighty God" and "prince of peace".

"Peace"

The angel is very excited for God's people! He helps the shepherds find Jesus because Jesus brings peace with God. Jesus can make them live with God again.

★ ★ ★ ★ ★

What good news do the shepherds hear?

Wise men visit Jesus

Jesus' birth causes a stir. Stargazers in the east see a star rise in the sky and come to Jerusalem to ask where the king of the Jews will be born. They meet King Herod.

BEHIND THE SCENES WITH THE WISE MEN!

<<< FLASHBACK

... to Micah (page 93). Jesus is born in Bethlehem. Micah said a ruler descended from Abraham and David will be born there.

Script: Worshipping the King

THREE WISE MEN

Where has the king of the Jews been born? We saw his star!

HEROD (KING OF JUDEA)

(Worried, speaking to chief priests and teachers.)

Where will the Christ be born?

CHIEF PRIESTS AND TEACHERS

In Bethlehem! The prophet said, "Bethlehem! O small village! A ruler will come from you, from the distant past."

HEROD

(Secretly speaking to wise men.)

Go and find the boy. Tell me where you find him so I can worship him too.

THREE WISE MEN

(Following star to Bethlehem. Finding the house.)

We bow down and worship you. Here are gifts: gold, frankincense, and myrrh.

A dream has told us not to return to Herod. Let's go home another way.

(Return home a different way.)

"Worship"

Jesus' birth causes two responses. The wise men love to worship Jesus, but Herod the Great is afraid of him. He wants to keep his power and not bow to God's king.

★ ★ ★ ★ ★

How do people respond to Jesus?

101

Jesus at the Temple

Mary and Joseph don't expect people's reaction to Jesus. They take him to the Temple twice and learn more about their son.

BEHIND THE SCENES WITH THE BOY JESUS!

Script: Seeing the King

SIMEON (MAN WHO LOVES GOD)

(God told him he would not die before seeing the Lord's Christ. The Spirit shows him Jesus. Finds and picks up Jesus. Praises God.)

Lord, you told me I would see the Christ before I die.

Now I have seen your saviour, who reveals you to all nations on earth.

(Mary and Joseph marvel.)

SIMEON

(Speaks to Mary and Joseph.)

This boy will reject and destroy many, but also accept and raise up others.

"Father's house"

Jesus knows he is the Son of God. He also knows that teaching his people is very important. He knows, even at the age of twelve, that he must serve his Father in heaven.

★ ★ ★ ★ ★

Why are Mary and Joseph amazed and confused?

Script: Hearing the King

JESUS (AGE TWELVE)

(Mary and Joseph have lost Jesus. He sits among the teachers.)

TEACHERS

We can't believe how much this boy understands!

MARY

Jesus! We've been searching for you for three days!
Son, why did you do this to us?

JESUS

Why search? Didn't you know I had to be in my Father's house?

(Joseph and Mary look confused.)

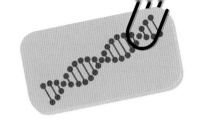

John baptizes Jesus

Twenty years later, John the Baptist is preparing the people. He is baptizing people to show how God's king can wash away sins. The people must prepare for their king.

BEHIND THE SCENES WITH JOHN THE BAPTIST!

Script: Awaiting the King

JOHN THE BAPTIST (JESUS' COUSIN)

(Calling to crowds. Crowds murmur together.)

Turn back to God! God's kingdom is near! Believe the good news!

Repent and God will forgive your sins!

Share your clothes! Share your food!

Tax collectors, don't collect more than you should!

Soldiers, don't take money by force. And be happy with your pay!

CROWD

(Wondering together.)

Is this man the Christ, the Messiah?

JOHN

I baptize you with water. But someone else will baptize you with the Holy Spirit!

(Jesus comes to the river.)

I need you to baptize me!

(Jesus disagrees. John baptizes Jesus.)

VOICE FROM HEAVEN

(Spirit descends like a dove onto Jesus.)

This is my Son. I love him and I am pleased with him.

"Repent!"

The people must "turn back" to God. They must be ready for God's kingdom because his king is here. God tells them that Jesus is their Messiah and his Son.

★ ★ ★ ★ ★

Why does John baptize the people?

103

SCENE 2: THE FRIEND OF SINNERS

Jesus gathers his first followers

Up north in Galilee, Jesus begins to gather followers: "Repent and believe the good news!" Society rejects most of his followers, but Jesus treats them like treasure.

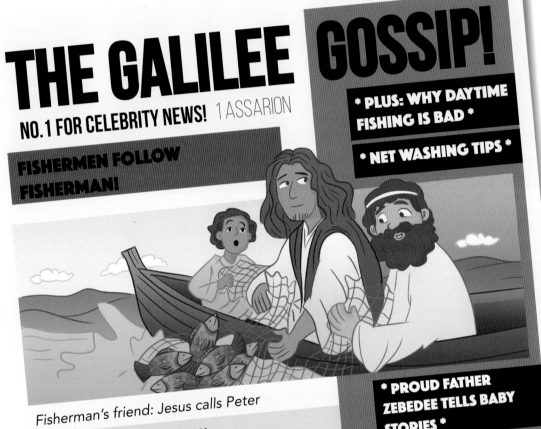

THE GALILEE GOSSIP!

NO. 1 FOR CELEBRITY NEWS! 1 ASSARION

FISHERMEN FOLLOW FISHERMAN!

* PLUS: WHY DAYTIME FISHING IS BAD *

* NET WASHING TIPS *

* PROUD FATHER ZEBEDEE TELLS BABY STORIES *

Fisherman's friend: Jesus calls Peter

JESUS FISHES FOR MEN!

CARPENTER JESUS catches fishermen. Jesus is walking along the shores of Lake Galilee when he sees Simon and his brother Andrew fishing.

"Follow me, and you will fish for people." We hear they immediately dropped their nets and followed him!

Jesus keeps walking along the beach and sees James and John, Zebedee's sons. They are fixing their nets. He calls them too, and they immediately leave their father and the men they hired! They follow Jesus too!

Some gossip says that Jesus even caught fish, enough to make two boats sink! More updates to follow.

"Follow me"

Jesus wants many followers. He tells his followers they will catch other followers too. They will turn back to God (repent) and follow their king.

★ ★ ★ ★ ★

How and why does Jesus gather followers?

Jesus gathers twelve disciples

Jesus shocks everyone with his choice of friends. The crowds want teaching and healing, but he gathers disciples (followers).

THE GALILEE GOSSIP!

NO. 1 FOR CELEBRITY NEWS! 1 ASSARION

JESUS COLLECTS TAX COLLECTOR FOR SERIOUS CHANGE

Money man: Jesus calls Levi

LEVI: FROM HATED TO HEALED

ENEMY OF the state Levi is a follower and friend of Jesus. Jesus walks through Capernaum and sees Levi at his tax-collecting booth. He's surrounded by stolen money. Giving our money to the Romans! Sickening traitor. Jesus says, "Follow me," and Levi follows him! No one expected this!

The story gets even richer. Jesus eats dinner with many tax collectors and sinners, and his disciples. Loads of people now follow him! The Pharisees (our teachers of the Law) ask the disciples, "Why does he eat with tax collectors and sinners?"

Jesus overhears and surprises everyone. "People who are healthy do not need a doctor, only the sick. I have not come to gather righteous people, but sinners."

REVEALED: JESUS CHOOSES TWELVE DISCIPLES!

Main men: twelve disciples

TWELVE TASKED with preaching and casting out demons. *THE GALILEE GOSSIP!* makes the list: Simon (Peter); James and John (the Sons of Thunder); Andrew, Philip, Bartholomew, Levi (Matthew), Thomas, James (son of Alphaeus), Thaddaeus, Simon the Zealot, and Judas Iscariot.

"Righteous people"

Jesus' friends know they need forgiveness. Only the sick think they need a doctor. Even though the Pharisees feel righteous and healthy, they still need forgiveness.

★ ★ ★ ★ ★

<<< FLASHBACK

… to Israel's twelve tribes (page 55). Jesus gathers twelve disciples because he wants a new twelve to lead his people.

Why do some people not like Jesus?

A foreign woman finds the Messiah

Jesus offers his people life to the full. He meets a foreign woman, a Samaritan. Normally Jews hate Samaritans, but Jesus changes her life for the better.

THE SAMARITAN SCOOP!

— STORIES THAT SHOCK • — • 1 ASSARION

| JESUS OFFERS LIVING WATER | LOCAL WOMAN'S SECRETS REVEALED | "I AM MESSIAH" SAYS JESUS |

WORLD EXCLUSIVE: MESSIAH OR MADMAN?

Shock moment: Jesus reveals all

Woman Calls Jesus Messiah

IT'S NOON at Jacob's well outside Sychar when our Samaritan woman meets Jesus. She is trying to avoid people! Maybe they hate her for being married five times.

Shock request! Jesus wants a drink. A Jewish man cannot talk to a Samaritan woman! Then he says, "If you knew who I am, you would ask for living water." But Jesus did not bring a bucket for the deep well! Where does he get living water?

Shock reply! "You will be thirsty again if you drink water from this well. You will never be thirsty again if you drink the water I give."

The woman says, "Give this water to me so I don't have to keep coming to this well." She is confused about living water.

Shock knowledge! Jesus knows her. "Bring your husband. No, the man you are with now is not your husband. You have had five!" How does he know? Is he a prophet?

Shock claim! She says, "The Messiah (the Christ) will explain!" But Jesus says, "I am he." She now tells the town, "Come, see who knows me, the saviour of the world!"

"Living water"
Jesus promises a satisfying friendship with God. He calls himself the Messiah and God himself, who lives with and rules his people forever. The water is eternal life.

★ ★ ★ ★ ★

What is Jesus offering?

Peter sees who Jesus is

Jesus wants to check who his disciples worship. He is in Caesarea Philippi, where many once worshipped gods like Baal, and now worship Greek gods like Pan.

2 ASSARII

REAL RELIGIOUS REPORTING

TEMPLE CHATTER!

HOT AND ANGRY EXCLUSIVE:
GALILEE MAN BLASPHEMES PAN

PLUS: ZEUS'S NEW TEMPLE

FIRST PHOTOS OF PAN'S GROTTO

PRIESTS POSE FOR FASHION SHOOT

Crazy claim: Jesus calls himself the Christ

Peter Calls Jesus Son of God

TEACHER JESUS is gathering opinion. He asks his disciples, "Who do people say I am?" His disciples give him the lowdown. "Some say you are John the Baptist. Others say you are a prophet like Elijah, back from heaven, or you are Jeremiah."

Then Jesus gets personal. "What about you? Who do you say I am?" Simon Peter, a fisherman from Galilee, is sure. "You are the Christ, the Son of the living God."

Jesus has plans for him. "Good for you! My Father showed this to you. And I say you are Peter, and you are the rock I will build my church on. Nothing will stop it." Jesus tells his disciples to tell no one he is the Christ.

"Son of the living God"

Peter knows why he follows Jesus. He calls Jesus the Chosen One (Christ). Jesus is God himself, the Son of God. Other gods are fake.

★ ★ ★ ★ ★

What does Peter believe?

Pharisees make Jesus an enemy

Jesus warns his friends against the religious leaders. The Pharisees were teachers of the Law, and find Jesus working on the day of rest (the sabbath).

2 ASSARII

REAL RELIGIOUS REPORTING

TEMPLE CHATTER!

LAWBREAKER JESUS WORKS ON THE SABBATH

CLAIM: "I AM LORD OF THE SABBATH"   PHARISEES LEFT STUNNED

No grain of truth: Jesus the liar

Jesus Takes on Pharisees in Grain Field Battle

LAST SABBATH Jesus took his disciples through a grain field, and they began to eat the heads of grain. We at *TEMPLE CHATTER!* know the sabbath is a day for no work! The Pharisees tell us so.

The Pharisees correct him. "Why are your followers breaking the law of the sabbath? They are working!" Jesus tells them about David.

"You should know that David ate the holy bread from the Temple. He was hungry, and he gave some to his friends too! The Law says only the priests can eat that bread!"

He says, "God made the sabbath to meet the needs of people. He did not make people to meet the laws of the sabbath. I am the Lord of the Sabbath." Many reports are emerging of Jesus disagreeing with the Pharisees. More to follow.

"Lord of the Sabbath"

Jesus says he made the Law and is in charge of it. He knows what it really means. But the Pharisees don't know and don't know who Jesus is.

★ ★ ★ ★ ★

What don't the Pharisees understand?

Jesus criticizes the Pharisees

Jesus wants everyone to see their own sin. The Pharisees, however, think they are good enough for God. Jesus warns others not to follow these religious teachers.

2 ASSARII

REAL RELIGIOUS REPORTING

TEMPLE CHATTER!

"CHILDREN OF HELL!"

JESUS MAKES WAR OF WORDS ON TRUSTED PHARISEES!

Words of warning: angry Jesus

Superstar Teacher Warns Against Learning From the Best

JESUS FORBIDS copying the teachers and Pharisees. "They preach, but do not practise what they preach." He calls them hypocrites: they are not what they seem.

He says Pharisees shut heaven's door in people's faces. They will not enter heaven and will stop others going too. "Hypocrites! You cross land and sea to make just one person copy you. And when they do, you make them twice a child of hell as you."

Jesus attacks their giving! "You give 10 per cent of your spices to the poor: mint, dill, and cumin! But you ignore more important things: fairness, mercy, faithfulness. Blind guides!" Jesus says they stretch out a fly, but shrink and swallow a camel!

Jesus has more names. "Hypocrites! You are clean on the outside, but dirty on the inside! Blind! Clean your heart first! You are whitewashed tombs! You look clean, but you are full of death. You look holy, but you are full of sin. Snakes and sons of vipers, you will not escape hell since you kill and crucify God's prophets."

ASK POPCORN SALLY

Does Jesus have enemies?

Yes and no. Jesus will rescue anyone, but many make him their enemy. In the book of Revelation, Jesus comes with a sword to strike down the people who reject him.

"Hypocrites!"

Jesus hates dishonesty. The Pharisees are hypocrites – they look perfect and teach the tiniest things in God's Law (flies), but they ignore the biggest things (camels).

★ ★ ★ ★ ★

What names does Jesus call the Pharisees?

SCENE 3: THE MAN OF SUPERPOWERS

Jesus makes wine

Jesus chooses a wedding feast to perform his first miracle. Nobody knows who he really is or what he can do. He is ready to answer these questions.

WEDDING A DISASTER WITHOUT WINE

WINNING WINE FROM WASHING WATER!

FEAST MASTER CALLS BRIDEGROOM GENIUS

SERVANTS CLAIM MIRACLE!

GALILEE GUEST GETS GLORY

IN CANA last week, a wedding turns to tragedy when the wine runs out. At first, no one knows. Reports say a local man is told by his mother, "The wine has run out."

The man is called Jesus and hails from Nazareth, a few miles away. His disciples are with him. Jesus tells his mother, "My hour has not yet come." What does he mean?

Locals say his mother is called Mary. She told the wedding servants, "Do what Jesus says." Jesus sees six stone water jars used for washing. Each holds 20 to 30 gallons.

Jesus tells them, "Fill the jars with water." Will Jesus give out water now?

Miracle moment! The servants claim Jesus turned water into wine. He told them, "Take out some water and give it to the master of the feast." They do it and the master is shocked. Water? No! He tastes wine. Reports claim no swap or mix-up.

The master of the feast tells the bridegroom. Neither has a clue. "At weddings, the best wine is served first. But you saved the best wine until last."

The servants are telling everyone. They say this Jesus showed his "glory". The man's disciples now believe in him. THE GALILEE GAZETTE will follow him.

"My hour has not yet come"

Jesus is planning a greater wedding feast. But first he must die, which he calls his "hour". He will celebrate later when he lives with his people in the new creation.

★ ★ ★ ★ ★

What is Jesus showing?

Jesus forgives a paralysed man

Jesus wants to show he can forgive sins. In Capernaum a whole town comes to hear him. The house is full, and one man wants to be healed...

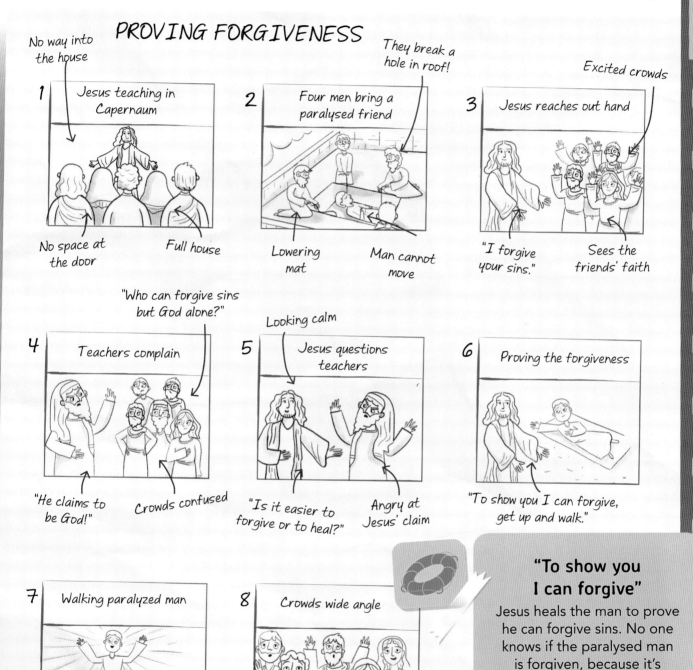

PROVING FORGIVENESS

No way into the house

1 — Jesus teaching in Capernaum

No space at the door

Full house

They break a hole in roof!

2 — Four men bring a paralysed friend

Lowering mat

Man cannot move

Excited crowds

3 — Jesus reaches out hand

"I forgive your sins."

Sees the friends' faith

"Who can forgive sins but God alone?"

4 — Teachers complain

"He claims to be God!"

Crowds confused

Looking calm

5 — Jesus questions teachers

"Is it easier to forgive or to heal?"

Angry at Jesus' claim

6 — Proving the forgiveness

"To show you I can forgive, get up and walk."

7 — Walking paralyzed man

Face glows with joy

Walks out in front of everyone

8 — Crowds wide angle

Amazed faces

"Never have we seen anything like this!"

Praising God

"To show you I can forgive"

Jesus heals the man to prove he can forgive sins. No one knows if the paralysed man is forgiven, because it's invisible. But when the man stands, everyone knows.

★ ★ ★ ★ ★

Why does Jesus heal the paralysed man?

Jesus calms a storm

Jesus finds another way to show who he is. His followers see and hear a lot of teaching, but they don't really understand who Jesus is. Then comes a terrifying storm…

FEAR OF DEATH TO TERROR OF TEACHER

SHOUT SILENCES STORMY SEAS

MAN CONTROLS STORM "WITH WORDS"

WHO IS JESUS? MAN OR GOD?

FISHERMEN CLAIM TEACHER IS GOD

LAKE GALILEE is known for violent storms. A man has stopped one of these storms, THE GALILEE GAZETTE reports.

Just days ago, a local man called Jesus was teaching by the sea. He told his disciples (some were fishermen) to cross to the other side. Eyewitnesses report that they left in the boat he was teaching in and other boats joined him.

That evening a massive storm comes and smashes over the boats, filling them with water. Witnesses say Jesus was sleeping in the stern. His disciples wake him and shout, "Teacher, don't you care if we drown?"

Jesus stands up and speaks to the sea itself! "Quiet! Be still!" Reports say the wind stopped and everything went calm at once. The man turns to his followers, "Why are you afraid? Do you still not believe?"

Now the disciples are terrified of Jesus. They say to each other, "Who is this? Even the wind and the waves obey him."

"Who is this?"

The disciples start to see who Jesus is. They call him teacher and then aren't sure. Teachers can't control storms! The storm scares them, but Jesus terrifies them!

★ ★ ★ ★ ★

Why are the disciples terrified?

Jesus feeds thousands

Jesus meets his people's needs. Massive crowds follow him to a faraway place and he calls them sheep without a shepherd. Soon a lot of people need feeding!

OH BOY! TINY MEAL FEEDS THOUSANDS!

GET A LOAF OF THIS! JESUS SHARES SNACK WITH THOUSANDS

5,000 REASONS JESUS IS AMAZING!

MIRACLE MAN MULTIPLIES MEAL

A TEACHER from Galilee feeds thousands. THE GALILEE GAZETTE has it all.

Reports say Jesus was sailing for a quiet place, but crowds of people saw him go and thousands ran on foot from the local towns to beat him there. We hear 5,000 followed, plus women and children. They say he stopped to teach them because they looked "like sheep needing a shepherd".

It got late and the disciples became worried. They were in a far-off place and the people ran there without food. The disciples wanted Jesus to send them home for food, but the gossip is that Jesus wanted his disciples to feed them. That would cost about 200 days' wages!

Jesus tells his disciples to find food, so they bring a boy's packed lunch! Five loaves and two fish... Jesus seats the crowd in groups. They're all waiting. What next? Jesus looks up to heaven and thanks God for the food. He then breaks the five loaves and hands them to his disciples to hand out. Then he splits up the two fish.

And everyone ate! To bursting! They picked up TWELVE BASKETFULS of leftovers! There are more than 5,000 as witnesses, plus families!

"Shepherd"

Jesus leads his people like a good shepherd. They wander after him, and he feeds them God's word as well as bread and fish. He satisfies all their needs.

★ ★ ★ ★ ★

<<< FLASHBACK

... to the desert (page 50). Jesus miraculously feeds the 5,000 in a faraway place, and God miraculously fed Israel honey bread in the desert.

How does Jesus satisfy the people?

Jesus raises Lazarus

Jesus uses death in his plan. His friend Lazarus is dying and his sisters beg for help.
He doesn't go, and two days later Lazarus dies. Jesus says, "Lazarus is asleep."

BUILDING BELIEF

1 Leaving for Bethany

Excited faces

"It's good I wasn't there. Now you will believe!"

2 Martha close-up

Not crying

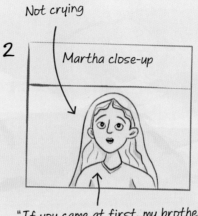

"If you came at first, my brother Lazarus would have lived!"

3 Jesus and Martha

"Lazarus will rise again."

"I know. At the resurrection of the dead."

Calming hand

4 Martha close-up

"I believe you are The Christ."

"You are the Son of God!"

5 Mary arrives

Crying at his feet

"If you came before, Lazarus would have lived!"

Jesus weeps. "Where is he?"

6 Cave wide angle

"Move the stone." Stone across tomb

"It will smell! He's been dead four days!"

7 Jesus prays close-up

"Father, I want them to believe."

"Lazarus, come out!"

8 Cave wide angle

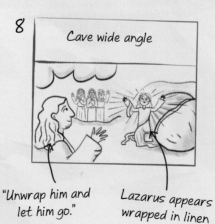

"Unwrap him and let him go."

Lazarus appears wrapped in linen

"Now you will believe"

Jesus lets Lazarus die to help the crowds believe. He raises Lazarus and calls himself the resurrection, because anyone who believes in him can have new life.

★ ★ ★ ★ ★

Why does Jesus call himself the resurrection?

Jesus' glory is unveiled

Three of Jesus' disciples catch a glimpse of who Jesus really is. Jesus takes Peter, and James and John up a mountain, but the next miracle happens to Jesus!

BRIGHT LIGHT AT NIGHT EXPLAINED!

FISHERMEN REPORT SEEING ELIJAH AND MOSES

SECRET UNTIL NOW: JESUS IS GOD'S SON

GOD SPEAKS AS JESUS MEETS ANCIENT PROPHETS

MONTHS AGO, Jesus met Elijah and Moses on a nearby mountain, THE GALILEE GAZETTE explains.

Witnesses have kept it secret until now, but Peter, James, and John have been telling others. Reports about Jesus' life are spreading around the area.

One night Jesus led his three friends up a high mountain near here. They say he became transfigured there. Experts say this means he suddenly looked different. His figure changed. His disciples say his clothes became shining white and some say no one has seen such whiteness. Until now.

That was when Elijah and Moses appeared, and they talked with Jesus. Peter thought they were staying around: "Teacher, this is great! We'll make tents for you all. One each!" Reports say that Peter was terrified and didn't know what else to say.

It goes on! A cloud then surrounds them all and a voice speaks from the cloud, "This is my Son, whom I love. Listen to him." And suddenly, the two prophets were gone. Jesus told them to keep the transfiguration secret. Months on, the stories are out.

<<< FLASHBACK

… to the tabernacle and Temple (pages 46, 69). A cloud surrounds them, like how a cloud of God's glory surrounds the priests. Jesus' changed figure shows them his glory.

"Shining white"

Jesus shows his eternal glory. His figure changes (transfigures), his clothes glow, and he dazzles his disciples with the glory he had and will have in the new creation.

★ ★ ★ ★ ★

What do the disciples glimpse about Jesus?

Jesus heals Blind Bartimaeus

It's a surprise who recognizes Jesus. Over in Jericho, crowds of people are following Jesus, but it seems only one man sees his special title.

SEEING THE SON OF DAVID

Disciples follow

1 Jesus leaves Jericho

Massive crowd follows

2 Bartimaeus, blind beggar

Desperate

"Jesus, Son of David, have mercy on me!"

3 Crowds shouting back

Many ignore man

"Shut up, old man!"

No one stops

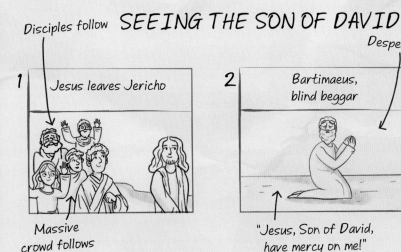
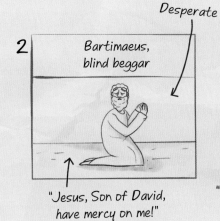

4 Bartimaeus close-up

"Son of David, have mercy on me!"

5 Jesus calling

"Call him over."

"Cheer up! Come on, he's calling you!"

6 Jesus close-up

Bartimaeus springs over

"What would you like me to do?"

7 Bartimaeus close-up

Standing

"Teacher, I want to see again."

Looking in general direction

8 Healing

"Go! Your faith has healed you!"

Bartimaeus sees and follows Jesus

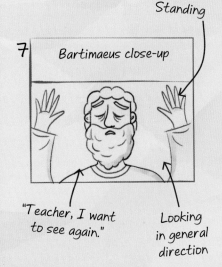

"Son of David"

The blind man sees and the crowd is blind. Bartimaeus knows that Jesus is the "Son of David", God's eternal king. People don't need to see Jesus in person to believe.

★ ★ ★ ★ ★

How are Bartimaeus and the crowd different?

Jesus explains his power over demons

Jesus shows what the Christ will do. God promised a snake crusher to defeat the devil, so when he casts out a demon, the crowds wonder, "Is he the Christ?"

JESUS CASTS AWAY DEMONS AND DOUBT

IS THIS THE SON OF DAVID?

PHARISEES: JESUS IS THE DEVIL!

JESUS CLAIMS GOD'S POWER AFTER DEMON-CASTING

ANOTHER demon-possessed man has been healed, prompting fresh questions about who Jesus is. THE GALILEE GAZETTE investigates once more.

The crowds want to see a healing. They bring a man with an evil spirit that made him blind and mute. Jesus heals him and the crowds ask, "Is this the Son of David?"

The Pharisees overhear the crowds and claim he has the devil's power. "Satan, the prince of demons, gives him the power to cast out demons!"

Jesus knows what they're thinking and explains. "If a kingdom attacks itself, then it will fall. And if Satan casts out Satan, he is attacking himself! Then surely he makes his own kingdom fall?"

He continues, "But if I cast out demons with God's Spirit, then God's kingdom has arrived. Who can raid Satan's house and tie him up?"

"Tie him up"

Jesus reveals the Christ's (Messiah's) power to defeat the devil. The crowds want a warrior like King David, but Jesus will rescue them from sin and death.

★ ★ ★ ★ ★

ASK 3D FREDDIE

What is God's kingdom?

It's when people treat Jesus as king. Many people today know Jesus as king, but in the new creation they will love their king perfectly.

Why can Jesus cast out demons?

SCENE 4: THE PREACHER OF PARABLES

On prayer

The people misunderstand prayer and need a teacher. Every day, Jesus prays alone to his Father in heaven, but the people show off their prayers to others.

Script: Speaking to God

JESUS
(Seeing the crowds, Jesus goes onto a mountain and sits.)
(His disciples join him.)
When you pray, do not copy the hypocrites! They love to pray in front of people, in the Jewish synagogues, and on street corners. In fact, they get the reward they want.

You should pray away from others. Go inside and shut your door! Then pray to your Father, who will see you and reward you.

When you pray, don't babble on with lots of words. Your Father knows what you need before you ask him!

Pray like this:

Our Father in heaven,
high and holy is your name.
May your kingdom come,
and what you want be done,
here on earth just like it is in heaven.
Give us today what we really need,
and forgive us our wrongs
as we forgive those who wrong us.
Help us not be tempted,
but keep us from evil.

"Father in heaven"
Jesus explains how to trust God. They should remember that God knows what they need, and ask him for help as their Father. This is the Lord's Prayer.

★ ★ ★ ★ ★

What does Jesus teach about prayer?

On God's kingdom

Jesus gives pictures of God's kingdom. He says, "The kingdom of God is near!" This kingdom is made of people who treat Jesus as king. He explains...

Script: The Kingdom of God

JESUS

(Teaching crowds of people)

The kingdom of God is like a tiny mustard seed that a man planted in his field. It's smaller than any other seed, but becomes bigger than any other tree. Even the birds come and nest in its branches.

And the kingdom of God is like buried treasure, buried in a field. A man finds it and covers it again. Then he joyfully sells everything he has to buy the field and get the treasure.

Again, the kingdom of God is like a fine pearl. A trader searches everywhere for it and, when he finds it, he sells all he has to buy it.

Again, the kingdom of God is like a net that gathers all kinds of fish. When it's full, men bring it in and divide the good from the bad. The end of time is like this. Angels will divide good and evil people, who they throw into the fire.

PHARISEES

When will the kingdom of God come?

JESUS

You cannot see the kingdom come. It's coming, but no one can say, "Look, there!" Listen, the kingdom is already here among you. Very soon, you will want to see me, but you won't see me.

People will say, "Look, there he is! There!"

Do not listen to them. You will see me like the lightning that flashes and lights up the whole sky.

Before that, I must suffer terribly and people will reject me.

"Already here"

The kingdom grows like a seed, is priceless like treasure, and gathers in many people. It starts on earth and continues when Jesus returns to make all things new.

★ ★ ★ ★ ★

What does Jesus teach about God's kingdom?

LUKE 10

On loving enemies

Jesus gives a lesson on who to love. A man thinks he loves his neighbours and is showing off about it. He asks, "Who is my neighbour?" and Jesus shows him.

Script: The Good Samaritan

JEWISH TRAVELLER
(Walks along. Sees some robbers.)
Oh no, stop, please! Don't hurt me!

ROBBERS
(Grab, smash, and punch. They strip him.)
I've got his **clo**thes! Let's run — he looks pretty dead!

PRIEST
(Walks along. Sees the man.)
Urghh! I'm staying away from you!
(Passes on far side of the road.)

LEVITE
(Priest's assistant arrives. Sees the man.)
What's that? Is he dead? I'm staying away!
(Passes on far side of the road.)

SAMARITAN
(Foreign enemy arrives. Sees the man and runs to him.)
Oh my! Let me bandage your wounds. This oil and wine will help. Take my own animal. I'll get you to an inn.
(Leads donkey to an inn.)
Innkeeper, here are two days' wages. Take good care of him for as long as he needs, and when I return I will pay you back any extra costs.

"Samaritan"
The injured man's enemy is his neighbour! Jesus' listeners hate Samaritans, but only the Samaritan behaves like a neighbour. Jesus teaches to love everyone, just like him.

★ ★ ★ ★ ★

How should Jesus' listeners behave?

120

On how God accepts people

Jesus shows how to become God's friend. His parable will surprise everyone, because people expect to go to heaven by being good.

Script: The Pharisee and the Tax Collector

(Two men go to the Temple to pray.)

PHARISEE

(Stands by himself and prays.)

God, I thank you I am different from others, like robbers, unfair men, men who cheat on their wives, and that tax collector.

I fast twice a week, not once per year.

I give away 10 per cent of everything I get, not just my crops.

TAX COLLECTOR

(Stands far away.)

(Cannot look up to heaven.)

(Beats his chest.)

God, have mercy on me. I am a sinner.

(Tax collector goes home, accepted by God.)

(Pharisee is not accepted by God.)

JESUS

Everyone who lifts themselves up
God will lay low.
Everyone who lays themselves low
God will lift up.

"Mercy"

Both men need mercy! Jesus teaches that good deeds are not enough. Both need to admit sins and ask for forgiveness, but only one does. Heaven is a gift not a reward.

★ ★ ★ ★ ★

Why does God accept the tax collector, not the Pharisee?

On God finding lost people

Jesus explains how God feels when someone becomes his friend. At the time, only the unpopular people are accepting Jesus. The Pharisees only grumble.

Script: The Lost Sheep

SHEPHERD

(Looking around. Counts his 100 sheep.)
… 98. 99…
Where's the hundredth? It's not here!!
I've lost a sheep!
(Leaves the 99 in the open fields.)
I must find that lost sheep.
In fact, I won't give up until I find it.
(Searches everywhere.)
I'll find you if it's the last thing I do.
(Spots the lost sheep. Carries it home.)
There you are! I can't believe it. What joy!
(Gathers his friends.)
Celebrate with me! I found my lost sheep!

Script: The Lost Coin

(A woman has ten coins.)

WOMAN

Hold on! I've lost one. Where's that coin gone?
(Lights up the room. Searches very carefully.)
I will find you, coin.
(Finds the lost coin.)
There! Haha! Friends, come rejoice with me!
I found my lost coin!

"Celebrate!"

God celebrates when he is joined up with his people again. The shepherd finds lost sheep like God finds lost people. Jesus shows how important they are to God.

★ ★ ★ ★ ★

Why does God celebrate?

On God's generosity

Jesus tells a story about lost sinners finding God's love. The father is God, his younger son is like a "lost" sinner, and his older son is like a "perfect" Pharisee.

Script: The Lost Son

YOUNGER SON

Father, give me my inheritance now! That's half of your money!

(Takes, runs faraway, and spends it all. Has to feed pigs.)

Mercy! Even my father's servants have a better life than this!

FATHER

(Watching out. Sees son and runs to him.)

(Hugs and kisses son.)

YOUNGER SON

Father, I have sinned. I do not deserve to be your son. Make me like a hired servant…

FATHER

Quick, servants! Bring the best clothes. Bring a ring! Give him shoes and kill the fatted calf!

Let's celebrate! My son was lost, and now is found!

OLDER SON

(Comes near. Hears music and dancing. Asks servant what's happening.)

(Angry. Will not enter. Father comes to him.)

I've slaved for you for years! I never disobeyed, but you never gave me even a young goat for me and my friends. Yet you gave this son of yours a fattened calf!

FATHER

Son, we had to celebrate. Your brother was dead, and is now alive. He was lost, but is now found.

"Give him!"

God is very generous. He gives lost sinners a huge welcome because they turn back to him, and he tells people already with him to find his generous love too.

How is the father generous?

On Jesus the shepherd

Jesus is planning something different. The people want a warrior king, a Christ to rescue them from the Romans, but Jesus is a shepherd king.

Script: The Good Shepherd

JESUS

Imagine a sheep pen. Whoever does not enter through the door is a thief and a robber. But whoever enters by the door is the shepherd of the sheep. He knows their names and leads them out.

I am the door for the sheep. Others are thieves and robbers and sheep don't listen to them. I am the door. Whoever enters the sheep pen by me will be saved. A thief steals, kills, and takes life. But I came to give life — life complete with meaning and joy.

I am the good shepherd. I am ready to die for my sheep. Others do not die for their sheep. I am the good shepherd. I know my sheep and they know me.

I will bring sheep from another sheep pen and they will follow me too. Then there will be one flock and one shepherd.

My Father loves me because I am willing to die for my sheep. I lay down my life, and I will have it back again.

"Lay down"

Jesus is a perfect leader. He knows his people by name and he gives them life. Shepherds do not die for their sheep, but Jesus will die for them and return to life.

★ ★ ★ ★ ★

FLASH-FORWARD ▸▸▸

… to Gentile followers (page 143). Non-Jewish people from all over the world will follow Jesus. They are sheep from other sheep pens.

Why is Jesus the Good Shepherd?

On killing God's Son

Jesus knows he has enemies. The religious leaders are plotting to kill him, so he tells a story about their rebellion against the king. They will kill God's Son.

Script: The Farmers

VINEYARD OWNER

(Plants a vineyard. Sets up a fence, a winepress, and a tower.)
Here, men, I'm going away. Rent this vineyard and have a share of its harvest.

SERVANT 1

Farmers, it's harvest. The vineyard owner sent me to collect fruit.
(Farmers take and beat him.)

FARMERS (TOGETHER)

Scram! It's all ours! And don't come back!

SERVANT 2

Farmers, the vineyard owner sent me to…
(Farmers hit him on the head. Treat him awfully.)

FARMERS (TOGETHER)

Scram! No more of you! You'll learn!

SERVANT 3

Farmers, the vineyard owner…
(Farmers kill him. More servants come. Farmers beat or kill them.)

VINEYARD OWNER

I can send one more. My son. They will respect him.

FARMERS (TOGETHER)

Look! The heir! Let's kill him and the vineyard will be ours!
(Son arrives. Farmers kill him. Owner comes to kill farmers.)

ASK POPCORN SALLY

Aren't parables just confusing?

Meaningful, yes. Confusing, no. Just think simply. Who do the people represent? What is the big idea? Jesus wants people to think hard so the stories will become meaningful to them.

"The heir!"
Jesus accuses the rebellious leaders of wanting God's world for themselves. They should love God, but they kill his servants (prophets) and heir (Jesus).

★ ★ ★ ★ ★

What does Jesus teach about the religious leaders?

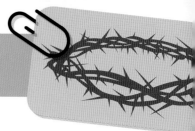

SCENE 5: THE SERVANT OF MANY

Jesus' plan

Everyone expects a warrior king. They think the Christ will rule Israel from Jerusalem, but Jesus will be a suffering king and he keeps repeating his plan.

Planning Meeting #1

Jesus   I must suffer a lot of awful things.

And then the elders, chief priests, and teachers will reject me.

Then I will be killed and I will rise again on the third day.

Peter   No, Jesus. That is plain WRONG! You are the Christ!

Jesus   Get away, Satan! You are not thinking about God's plan, but your own.

Planning Meeting #2

Jesus   I will be handed over into men's hands.

They will kill me, but I will rise again on the third day.

(Everyone looks confused. No one understands.)

(The disciples look afraid to ask Jesus about it.)

Planning Meeting #3

Jesus   We are going to Jerusalem.

There I will be handed over to the chief priests and teachers.

They will decide to kill me and hand me over to the Gentiles (non-Jews).

They will mock and spit on, flog and kill me. But I will rise on the third day.

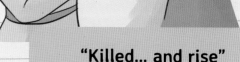

"Killed... and rise"

Jesus sees a different enemy to the people. They want their Christ to defeat the Romans, but Jesus will die and "rise again to defeat sin and death".

★ ★ ★ ★ ★

Why are Jesus' disciples confused?

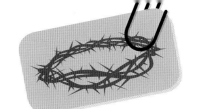

James and John's plan

Jesus' disciples want fame and power. They don't understand what Jesus means to "be killed and rise". Instead, they begin making their own plans.

Planning Meeting #3 (continued...)

James and John	Jesus, we want you to do whatever we ask. Allow us to sit each side of your glorious throne in Jerusalem.
	One on your right and the other on your left.
Jesus	James and John, you don't understand what you're asking for.
	Do you think you can go through what I will go through?
James and John	Yes we can!
Jesus	You will go through it, but someone else will choose who sits beside me.

(The other ten disciples are angry at James and John.)

Jesus	Look, all twelve of you. See the rulers of the Gentiles...
	They love to show off their power over others and their leaders command others.
	You should be different!
	If you want to be great, you should be a servant.
	If you want to be first, you should be the slave of everyone.
	Even I came not to be served but to serve others, and to give my life to save many.

"To save many"

Jesus is the servant of many. Jesus explains that true greatness is not about fame and power, but about being a servant leader. Jesus will even die to serve and save.

★ ★ ★ ★ ★

What don't James and John understand?

A triumphant entry into Jerusalem

Jesus rides into Jerusalem like a king, but he is a different kind of king. Instead of riding in on a horse of war, he chooses the animal of a servant.

On-Set Diary: Disciples

Why a donkey? Jesus sent two of us into the village and said we would immediately find a young donkey, a colt, which no one has ever ridden. We should untie it and bring it to him. If anyone asks questions, we should say, "The Lord needs it."

The prophet Zechariah said this would happen: "Rejoice, Jerusalem! Your king is coming! He rides lowly and victorious on a young donkey, a colt."

On-Set Diary: Crowds

The crowds were heaving! Jesus came through the city gates riding a colt, and people were laying cloaks on the ground, and even palm branches! Those palm branches are a symbol of victory for Israel. Jesus is coming for a victory!

We sang, "HOSANNA! Save us, O Son of David! God has blessed him to come! HOSANNA! Save us, O God." The whole city knew about it! But some people asked, "Who is he?" We hear he is the prophet Jesus, from Nazareth in Galilee!

On-Set Diary: Pharisees

Jesus has lost control! We told him, "Teacher, tell your disciples to be quiet!" He is not a saviour! But Jesus told us, "If they are quiet, the city stones will cry out!"

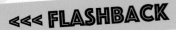

<<< FLASHBACK

… to Zechariah (page 94). Jesus enters Jerusalem just like Zechariah said, riding on a donkey lowly and victorious.

"Hosanna!"

Hosanna means "save us!" They want the Son of David (the Messiah or Christ) to save them. Jesus is planning to save them! But not the way they think.

★ ★ ★ ★ ★

Why doesn't Jesus choose a horse of war?

Bread and wine: rescue reminders

Jesus gives some final lessons. One Thursday night, at his Last Supper, he teaches his disciples to remember his body and blood, to remember how he serves them.

On-Set Diary: Matthew

The bread is his body?! We were meant to be celebrating the Passover! Jesus said, "Take this and eat it. This is my body, which I give for you."

Then Jesus thanked God for the wine and said, "Drink this wine. Everyone! This is my blood, which I will pour out for many people. It stands for the new covenant." Is Jesus starting a new agreement with God?!

On-Set Diary: John

Strange! What's Jesus doing?! Normally at feasts, a non-Jewish slave washes our feet when we arrive. But this time Jesus did it! He took off his robe, picked up a towel, and started washing our feet! Jesus! Not a slave!

Peter refused: "Lord, you will never wash my feet!" But Jesus said, "If I don't wash your feet, then you don't belong to me." Peter jumped. "Then wash my head and my hands too!" Jesus taught us to wash each other's feet. Love each other like servants!

On-Set Diary: Peter

Betray him? I had to know who he meant! Jesus said that one of us would betray him! I nodded at John to ask, "Lord, who?!" Jesus told him, "The person who I give this bread to after dipping it." He gave it to... Judas Iscariot! Then Judas slipped away.

Who would betray Jesus? I said, "Jesus, I would die for you!" He said to me, "Will you? Tonight, before the rooster crows, you will deny you know me three times."

"Body and blood"

Jesus gives rescue reminders. Broken bread reminds everyone of his broken body, and wine reminds them of his life poured out. Even the betrayer Judas should remember!

★ ★ ★ ★ ★

What are the disciples learning?

Jesus' last prayers

Jesus is getting ready. Ready to suffer. But he knows it's more than physical suffering. He's getting ready for his Father's anger, and he chooses it.

Location: Clearing for Final Prayers

Jesus Father, if you are willing, please take this cup away from me. May what you want be done, not what I want.

Prop: Cup of God's Anger

God holds a cup full of foaming, well-mixed wine.
He pours it out and the wicked drink it all, down to the dregs.

Prop: Sweat Like Blood

Jesus prays in agony.
He is so distressed that his sweat drops are like blood.

Location: Trees to Sleep Under

Jesus Why do you sleep at a time like this? Pray! Your spirit is willing, but your body is weak.

"Cup"

Soon Jesus will suffer God's anger. He expects to drink it down like wine in a cup: all God's anger for all of God's people across history. It agonizes him deeply.

★ ★ ★ ★ ★

Why is Jesus so distressed?

Jesus is found guilty

The same night, Jesus is sent to his death. Judas returns with a crowd of soldiers to arrest Jesus. He has six trials before they decide his crime: he claims to be God.

Prop: Clubs and Swords

Judas leads a crowd to arrest Jesus with clubs and swords.

Prop: High Priest's Chair

High priest hears lies about Jesus, and condemns him to death for claiming to be the Christ, the Son of God.

Prop: Courtyard Fire

Peter keeps warm and people say he is with Jesus, but he says three times he does not know him.

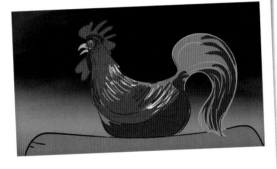

Prop: Rooster

The rooster crows immediately after Peter denies knowing Jesus.

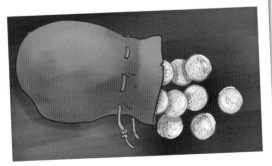

Prop: 30 Pieces of Silver

Judas changes his mind and throws the silver he was paid back to the chief priests, before hanging himself.

Prop: Bowl of Water

Pontius Pilate, the Roman governor, finds Jesus innocent. But the crowds force him to crucify Jesus, so he washes his hands in innocence.

"Death"

Everyone abandons Jesus. Judas betrays, Peter denies, the high priest accuses him of lying, and Pontius Pilate gives in to the crowd. Jesus will die for telling the truth.

★ ★ ★ ★ ★

Why will Jesus die?

131

Rejected (double bill)

The Romans and Jewish rulers reject Jesus. On the Friday, they crucify him at a place called "The Skull". They all mock, but they don't know what they are seeing.

Script

JESUS

Father, forgive them.
They don't know what they're doing.

JEWISH RULERS

Hah! He saved other people!
He should save himself if he is the Christ, God's Chosen One.

SOLDIERS

King of the Jews?! Then save yourself!

THIEF

Aren't you the Christ? Then save yourself and us!

THIEF 2

Hey, fear God! We deserve to die, but Jesus is innocent.
Jesus, remember me when you enter your kingdom.

JESUS

Trust me… Today you will be with me in paradise.

<<< FLASHBACK

… to a prophecy in Daniel (page 94). The anointed one will die with nothing.

"Hail the king of the Jews!"

"Here is the king of the Jews"

An earthquake splits rocks

"King… Save!"

Only one of the thieves sees what Jesus is doing. They mock "King Jesus" because he is dying instead of saving. But in fact, Jesus is saving them by dying.

★ ★ ★ ★ ★

Why does Jesus accept the second thief?

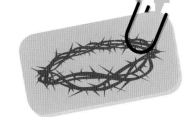

Rejected (double bill)

Darkness hangs overhead. God the Father is angry. However, he isn't rejecting the *people*, instead *Jesus* is being rejected by his Father. He is taking God's anger against their sin.

Darkness from midday until 3 p.m.

Temple curtain tears in two

Gambling for Jesus' clothes

<<< FLASHBACK

…to the temple curtain (page 69). It separated the sinful people from their holy God. When Jesus dies, the barrier is torn down. They can live with God again.

JESUS

(at 3 p.m.)

My God! My God! Why have you abandoned me?

JESUS

It is finished!

JESUS

Father, I give my spirit into your hands.

CENTURION

(Looks at Jesus.)

He really was the Son of God!

"It is finished!"

Jesus pays for people to be friends with God again. The word for "finished" also means "paid". He takes God's anger, pays for sin, and crushes the snake (the devil).

★ ★ ★ ★ ★

Why does God reject Jesus?

133

Resurrected (double bill)

Everyone makes sure Jesus is dead and buried. A soldier spears him to check he is dead, and the priests and Pharisees want to prevent anyone stealing his body.

JOSEPH OF ARIMATHEA

Governor Pilate, I have no right to Jesus' body, but may I bury it today, because tomorrow is the sabbath?

PONTIUS PILATE

Certainly, Joseph. Give him the burial he deserves.

Centurion! Give orders for this man to have Jesus' body.

JOSEPH OF ARIMATHEA

I bought this sheet of linen for him.

NICODEMUS

I bought these spices, weighing about 32 kg. Fit for a king.

JOSEPH OF ARIMATHEA

This tomb was meant for me.

It's cut into solid rock! Now let's roll this heavy stone against the entrance.

WOMEN

(*Watching, opposite the tomb, crying.*)

"Secure the tomb"

Jesus' secure tomb means no one can fake his resurrection. Jesus promised to rise, but the heavy stone and the guards and the seal all make this impossible.

★ ★ ★ ★ ★

How and why is Jesus' tomb secure?

CHIEF PRIESTS AND PHARISEES

(To Pontius Pilate.)

The imposter, Jesus, said he would rise after three days. Secure the tomb or his disciples may steal his body.

PONTIUS PILATE

Fine. Make the tomb as secure as possible. Take a squad of soldiers and seal it with a Roman seal.

Resurrected (double bill)

On the Sunday morning, some women approach the tomb. They normally lay spices on the bodies of the dead, but they are to have a very big surprise.

MARY AND OTHER WOMEN

Who will roll the stone away to let us lay these spices on his body?

ANGEL

Don't fear! You're looking for Jesus. He has risen! See where they laid him. Go, tell the disciples!

PETER

Where? Where? Where is he?

There's the sheet of linen! There's the face cloth!

JOHN

I believe!

(*Peter and John walk home.*)

JESUS

Woman, why are you crying?

MARY

Sir, gardener, if you took Jesus' body, tell me where you have put him.

JESUS

Mary!

MARY

Teacher!

JESUS

Tell the disciples I will soon ascend to our Father in heaven. Go!

"He has risen!"

Good news must spread! Jesus has defeated death! Now there is life after death for Jesus' followers! The angel and Jesus tell the disciples to spread the news.

★ ★ ★ ★ ★

Why is the resurrection good news?

135

Meeting the risen Jesus

That Sunday, Jesus begins to appear to his people. Stories get around about the man who was crucified and is risen. But his followers don't always recognize his new body!

On-Set Diary: Peter

I tell you! It's true! It's really true! We saw the linen sheet lying there. And we saw the face cloth, separate from the sheet. It's like Jesus passed through them! You say someone stole the body? Then why would they leave the expensive linen?

On-Set Diary: Matthew

Just after Cleopas told us everything, Jesus came in! Even though our doors were locked! He showed us the scars in his hands and side. It was really him! Really him!

On-Set Diary: Cleopas

We met Jesus on the road and he explained everything! We didn't recognize him!

Two of us journeyed to Emmaus, talking about Jesus' death. A man walked with us and asked why we were sad. We replied, "Everyone knows! It's awful! Jesus of Nazareth, a great prophet, was condemned to die by our own chief priests and rulers. We hoped he would save Israel, but they crucified him. And this morning women said they met angels and Jesus himself at the tomb! We went and saw no one!"

The man explained. "O foolish people! The prophets promised Jesus would rise! The Christ had to suffer and then enter his glory." He explained how Moses and all the prophets expected him. Our hearts were burning within us. But at supper we recognized him! When he thanked God for the bread, we saw it was Jesus himself. Then he disappeared!

"Hearts were burning"

The Old Testament all points to Jesus. Cleopas is overjoyed as he understands God's rescue plan to save the world through Jesus. The joy burns in his heart.

★ ★ ★ ★ ★

Why does the Old Testament excite Cleopas?

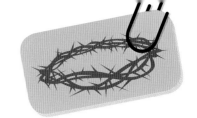

Even more meetings with Jesus

For 40 days, Jesus meets his disciples. On one occasion, he meets 500 people. Many believe that Jesus is alive, but Thomas doubts. He wants to see for himself.

On-Set Diary: Peter

We journeyed back to Lake Galilee to fish. Thomas, Nathanael, James and John, and two others were with us. Seven in all. We caught nothing.

At dawn a man spoke from the shore. "Have you caught anything?" He told us to cast our nets on the right side and suddenly fish filled the net! Too heavy to lift!

It was Jesus! I swam over to him and we cooked the fish. We had 153 big ones and they didn't even break the net! We all knew it was Jesus. No question at all. He asked three times, "Do you love me?" I said yes each time. "Feed my lambs," he replied. It upset me, because at his trials I had denied him three times, but he still accepts and loves me.

On-Set Diary: Thomas

What a funny day! It's like Jesus knew exactly what I said last Sunday! I had said, "Unless I touch the scars in his hands and side, I will not believe!" I was absolutely sure Jesus was not alive. The others imagined it! Days went by and I became even more sure. I thought: "If I'm going to believe, I need to see for myself!"

But today Jesus appeared! He said, "Touch the scars in my hands and side. Stop doubting and believe!" I said, "My Lord and my God." Jesus really is God himself! Jesus said, "You believed because you saw me for yourself. How truly blessed are those who do not see but still believe."

On-Set Diary: John

I wrote this good news so people will believe that Jesus is the Christ, the Son of God. Believing in him will give them new life.

"Believe!"

Believing brings new life. Thomas believes that Jesus defeated death, and John writes to help others believe. New life is about sins forgiven and living with Jesus forever.

★ ★ ★ ★ ★

What have the disciples learned about Jesus?

Geography: Jesus around Galilee

For about three years, Jesus performs miracles and teaches around Galilee. He visits many of its towns and villages, teaching the people about the kingdom of God.

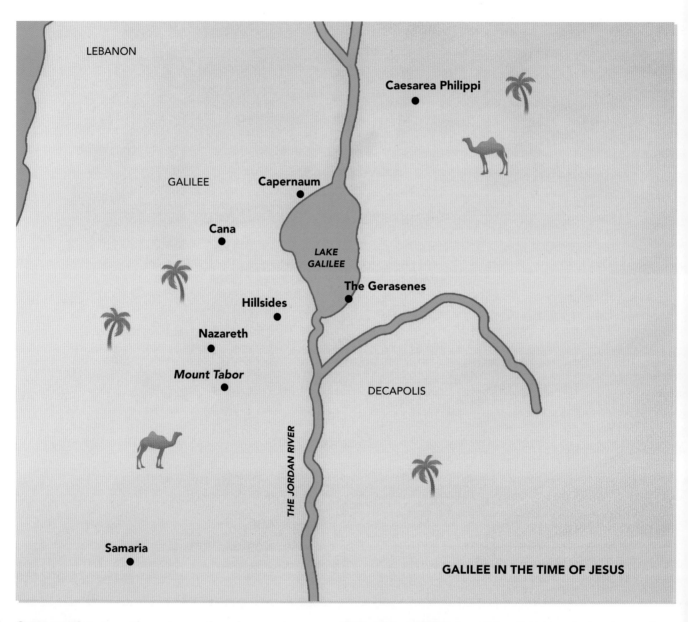

GALILEE IN THE TIME OF JESUS

- **Nazareth** is Jesus' hometown where he grew up as a carpenter.
- **The Jordan River** is where John the Baptist prepares the way for the Chosen One.
- **Capernaum** is Peter's hometown where Jesus meets Levi and the paralyzed man.
- **Lake Galilee** is a small freshwater lake, but can produce violent storms.
- **Samaria** is home to despised Samaritans like the woman at the well by Sychar.

- **Caesarea Philippi** worships Greek gods, but is where Peter calls Jesus the Christ.
- **Cana** is where Jesus attended a wedding and turned water into wine.
- **Hillsides** are perfect spots to teach big crowds, even as many as 20,000 people!
- **Mount Tabor** may be where Jesus was transfigured.
- **The Gerasenes** is where Jesus cast a man's evil spirits into a herd of pigs.

*Map not to scale

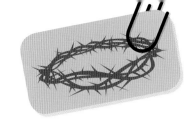

Geography: Jesus around Jerusalem

Jesus visits Jerusalem every year for the Passover festival, until he dies at Passover as the new Passover Lamb. The Romans rule Jerusalem as the region's capital.

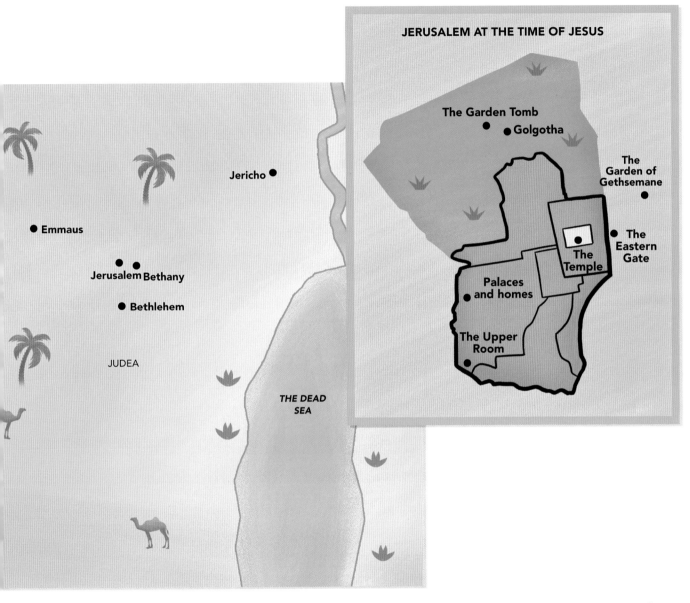

JERUSALEM AT THE TIME OF JESUS

The Garden Tomb
Golgotha
The Garden of Gethsemane
The Eastern Gate
The Temple
Palaces and homes
The Upper Room

Jericho
Emmaus
Jerusalem Bethany
Bethlehem
JUDEA
THE DEAD SEA

- **Bethlehem** is where Jesus was born in a stable and met wise men and shepherds.

- **The Temple** is where Jesus often taught and set the story of the Pharisee and the tax collector.

- **Jericho** is the home of Bartimaeus.

- **Bethany** is the home of Mary, Martha, and Lazarus.

- **The Eastern Gate** is where Jesus entered Jerusalem on a donkey.

- **The Upper Room** holds Jesus' Last Supper, where he gives bread and wine.

- **The Garden of Gethsemane** sat on the Mount of Olives, where Jesus prayed.

- **Palaces and homes** hold six trials for Jesus until Pontius Pilate sentences him.

- **Golgotha** means "The Place of the Skull" and is the hill where Jesus is crucified.

- **The Garden Tomb** belongs to Joseph of Arimathea but is used for Jesus.

- Road to **Emmaus** is where Cleopas and the other disciple meet the risen Jesus.

*Maps not to scale

ACT 7: GLOBAL GOSPEL

SCENE 1: GO, GO, GO!

Jesus gives final instructions

The news must spread in all directions. The camera now zooms out to the whole world! Jesus wants people everywhere to believe and have new life with him.

THE GREAT COMMISSION

1 **Jesus** God the Father has given me all power and command.

2 And so I command you: Go, go, go to all the nations and make disciples there!"

3 Baptize them and teach them to obey everything I have commanded you.

4 I promise you, I will be with you until the end of time."

THE ASCENSION

5 **Jesus** Stay in Jerusalem and wait for the gift my Father promised.

6 (Jesus ascends up into the sky and sits down at the right hand of God.)

7 (The disciples watch Jesus until a cloud hides him.)

8 **Two angels** You have seen Jesus ascend into heaven, but he will return in the same way you saw him go.

"Sits down"

Jesus sits down in heaven to rule as king. He has defeated sin and death. He promises to send his Spirit so he can be with all of his disciples as they continue his work.

★ ★ ★ ★ ★

FLASH-FORWARD >>>

... to Judgment Day (page 155). Jesus promises to return and judge all people with justice. He says only his Father knows when he will come.

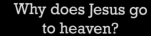

Why does Jesus go to heaven?

The Holy Spirit comes

Jesus has gone, but he has not left his people on their own. The Holy Spirit will help them spread the gospel (good news), and kick-start them with foreign languages!

PENTECOST

1 *(All the disciples are together.)*

2 *(A sudden sound like a powerful blowing wind fills the house.)*

3 *(Some flickers that look a bit like fire appear in the room.)*

4 *(The flickers rest over their heads.)*

5 *(The Holy Spirit fills the disciples, who speak foreign languages.)*

6 Disciples The Lord has risen! Jesus is the Christ!

7 Crowds They're from Galilee! How can they speak our languages?

8 Onlookers What does this mean?
Others They're drunk!

ASK POPCORN SALLY

Where should Jesus' followers go?

Everywhere! Jesus sends his followers to tell the good news to their families, and families everywhere on earth, in all nations.

<<< FLASHBACK

… to the Tower of Babel (page 21). God mixed up languages, and now reverses this. He wants people to understand the good news.

"Spirit"
God now lives inside his people! His Spirit gives them power to tell the gospel (good news), to believe it, and understand it. He is Jesus' Spirit.

★ ★ ★ ★ ★

Why does Jesus send his Spirit?

141

SCENE 2: NEW PREACHERS

Peter speaks back

Jesus renews his disciples to be preachers like him. His Spirit helps them do it. At Pentecost, onlookers call the disciples drunk, so Peter steps up to preach.

Script: Peter's First Sermon

PETER

You think we're drunk? It's only 9 a.m.!

The prophet Joel once said:

"God says: I will pour out my Spirit on all people.
Your people will speak what I tell them and see visions and dreams.
I will pour out my Spirit and people will speak my words.
God will save everyone who calls to the Lord."

Hear this! You know Jesus of Nazareth performed miracles.
But, as God planned, you crucified him and God raised him to life.

King David once said:
"I saw the Lord so I will live in hope.
You will not abandon me in death,
or let your Holy One rot in the grave."

Brothers, David was not talking about himself!
His body is still in his tomb!
He knew God's promise to him
and he talked about the resurrection of the Christ.
We have seen Jesus raised from the dead
and he has poured out his Spirit, as he promised.

KNOW THIS! God has made Jesus both Lord and Christ!
Turn back to God for forgiveness and be baptized,
God will give you the Holy Spirit too.

"Holy One"

The Spirit helps the disciples. He helps Peter explain the predictions about the coming of the Spirit and Jesus' resurrection. And he helps 3,000 people believe that day.

★ ★ ★ ★ ★

How does the Spirit help Peter and the crowd?

Peter meets Roman Cornelius

Soon there are Gentile (non-Jew) believers. North in Caesarea, there is a Roman centurion Cornelius who loves God, and an angel appears to him in a vision.

CITY CHAT

- ☐ PHOTOS
- ☺ FRIENDS
- ◔ EVENTS

@CAESAREA

Cornelius (3 days ago)

My trusted soldier! Go, now to Joppa and find Peter. An angel told me he is staying with Simon the tanner, who lives by the sea. Bring Peter here.

Peter (2 days ago)

Just had a vision. A great sheet came down from heaven. On it were all kinds of animals, reptiles, and birds. A voice said: "Rise, kill, and eat!" I called the food unclean for Jews, but the voice said, "Do not call unclean what God has made clean." All happened three times. Then the sheet went back up. Got me thinking!

Soldier (2 days ago)

The Spirit told Peter to let us in! Tomorrow he will join us in Caesarea.

Cornelius (today)

Peter, it's a good thing you had *your* vision! We know it is against your law to mix with Romans, so it's good news he told you not to call anyone unclean.

Peter (today)

The Holy Spirit helped me explain! I said, "I see that God accepts people from every nation, not just Jews. The Lord Jesus performed miracles, but he was crucified, raised from death, and appeared to many. And he sent us to explain that he will judge the living and the dead. God will forgive anyone who believes in him!"

Soldier (today)

That's not all! Then the Holy Spirit filled us Romans and we too spoke in other languages! God really does want non-Jews to follow him! He is good!

"God has made clean"

Forgiveness is also for Gentiles. God cleans Jews and non-Jews through Jesus' death. Now they are all equally forgiven. God's rescue plan is international.

★ ★ ★ ★ ★

How does God include Gentiles in his rescue?

Stephen is attacked

The Jewish rulers hate the disciples. They arrest Stephen for teaching about Jesus: "He spoke against Moses and God!" The Spirit helps him explain.

Script: The Stoning of Stephen

STEPHEN
Remember our history! Remember Abraham, Isaac, and Jacob.
Remember Joseph. Remember our people as slaves in Egypt.
Remember Moses, who led us to Mount Sinai,
but who was rejected when they built the golden calf.
Remember how God drove out our enemies before Joshua.
Remember David, who wanted to build God's Temple,
and remember how Solomon built it for him.
You stubborn and rebellious people!
You always battle against the Holy Spirit!
You are just like your ancestors,
who attacked and killed the prophets,
who promised the Righteous One.
You now betrayed and murdered him,
you who loved God's Law but never kept it.

HIGH PRIEST
(Grinding his teeth in rage.)

STEPHEN
(Looking up to heaven.)
I see heaven open, and Jesus standing at God's right hand.

COUNCIL OF RELIGIOUS LEADERS
Cover your ears! Cover your ears!
(Drag Stephen out of the city. Stone him to death.)

STEPHEN
Lord Jesus, receive my spirit and do not hold
this sin against them.

"Stubborn"

The Jewish rulers refuse to believe! And they are supposed to love God! They stubbornly reject Stephen like they rejected Jesus, but Stephen stubbornly believes.

★ ★ ★ ★ ★

Why do the religious leaders stone Stephen?

Philip and the Ethiopian

The attack on Stephen scatters the disciples. One disciple, Philip, preaches and heals many people – until an angel comes to him with a special job.

📷 SNAPSCROLL @THEROADTOGAZA

1 PHILIP

WOW! I JUST MET AN ANGEL! HE SAID, "GO SOUTH TO THE DESERT ROAD BETWEEN JERUSALEM AND GAZA." WHAT'S THERE?

2 PHILIP

HMMM. THIS CARRIAGE CARRIES A SERVANT OF THE QUEEN OF ETHIOPIA. THAT MAN CONTROLS ALL THE QUEEN'S TREASURE!

3 PHILIP

The Spirit said, "Go join him." Hey, what's he reading?

4 ETHIOPIAN

"A man was silent like a sheep to the slaughter. Justice was taken from him and he was killed."

5 ETHIOPIAN

Is he talking about himself or someone else?

6 PHILIP

"That's Isaiah talking about Jesus!" I explained all the good news about Jesus.

7 ETHIOPIAN

"LOOK! WATER! CAN I BE BAPTIZED?" PHILIP BAPTIZED ME RIGHT THERE, BUT WHEN I CAME OUT OF THE WATER HE WAS GONE!

8 PHILIP

WHERE AM I? THE SPIRIT TOOK ME AWAY TO AZOTUS! PRAISE GOD THAT THE ETHIOPIAN BELIEVED!

"The Spirit said"

The Spirit controls everything. Philip finds the Ethiopian while he's reading about Jesus. They pass a rare pool at the perfect moment. The Spirit vanishes Philip away.

★ ★ ★ ★ ★

How does the Spirit help Philip and the Ethiopian?

145

Saul's conversion

Jesus chooses a disciple for a very special job: Saul. He is a Pharisee, killing "followers of the Way" such as Stephen. Now, he's off to Damascus to arrest any others.

LIVESTREAM

LIVE @Damascus

1min ago Saul is now baptized A FOLLOWER OF THE WAY!

5mins ago Ananias is praying for Saul… "You saw the Lord Jesus on the road here. He has sent me to you. So be filled with the Holy Spirit!" He's not blind now! It looked like scales fell off his eyes. Amazing!

8mins ago Jesus gave Ananias a vision! "Find Saul at Judas' house on Straight Street. He had a vision of you healing his blindness. I have chosen him to teach my name to Gentiles, kings, and Jews!"

20mins ago Saul has had another vision! He is blind and has not eaten for three days, but Ananias, a follower of the Way, is coming to heal him!

3 days ago This killing mission is over. Saul is now blind and staggering around. He's not going to arrest any followers like this. His men heard the voice above but never saw anything else.

3 days ago Hold up! Saul has fallen off his horse and is seeing a light brighter than the sun! There is a voice! "Saul, why do you attack me? I am Jesus, who you are attacking. Go to the city and I will tell you what to do."

9 days ago Oh dear! Soon there won't be any followers of the Way in Damascus. Saul has the high priest's written permission to arrest them all! Surely Saul will stop people believing in Jesus soon!

"I have chosen him"

Jesus has big plans for Saul. Saul hated Jesus' followers, and then he becomes one! He will teach people, including kings, about Jesus all over the Mediterranean.

★ ★ ★ ★ ★

How and why does Jesus choose Saul?

146

Paul goes to Philippi

Saul begins to teach about Jesus. He travels the Mediterranean under his Greek name, Paul. In one town, a strange collection of people believe his teaching.

@PHILIPPI

PHOTOS

FRIENDS

EVENTS

Lydia

I came to sell purple goods, but I found Paul! The Lord opened my heart and I believed his teaching! Paul baptized me and my whole family. Thank you!

Paul

Nuisance! A demon-possessed slave girl in town keeps shouting, "These men serve the Most High God. They teach how to be saved!" What's worse, her owners make money off her fortune telling!

Slave girl Freedom! Paul cast out the spirit I had saying, "In Jesus' name, come out of her!"

Magistrates That girl's owners are furious, and us too! We Romans cannot accept these foreign beliefs, so we beat Paul and his friends and sent them to prison.

Jailer Fear not, they are safe in prison with me! Feet safely in the stocks!

Paul What a miracle! We were praying and singing at midnight, when there was an earthquake! The prison doors flew open and our chains fell off. The jailer thought we escaped and almost killed himself. But we stayed and explained how he could be saved. Now his whole family believe in Jesus and are baptized!

"Baptize"

Baptism shows what Christians believe. They believe that Jesus has washed their sins away like water. Lydia and the jailer can use it to explain their new beliefs.

★ ★ ★ ★ ★

Why does Paul baptize the believers?

Magistrates Paul and friends, leave our city! We hear you are Roman citizens? We apologize for beating you without a trial. It was wrong, but please leave Philippi!

Paul explains how Jesus saves

Paul writes at least thirteen long letters to churches around the Mediterranean. One letter to the Christians in Rome explains how they can be friends with God.

KINGDOM STUDIO DEAL LEGAL FORM

Selected parts

1.16–17   **This deal is good news!**
Good news! God saves everyone who believes, whoever they are.
God gives them his goodness if they only have faith.

1.18–20   **God's anger against humankind**
The world shows off God's eternal power and his perfection, and there is no excuse not to believe he exists.
God has shown himself to people, but they have ignored him.
Because of this, God has been rightly angry at all humankind.

3.9–18   **No one is good**
Not one person loves God. Everyone turns away from him.
Their mouths are like open graves – full of death.
Their words are like snake's poison – full of lies and attacks.
Their feet are quick, running to hurt and kill, and their eyes do not fear God.

3.22-25   **Goodness given by faith**
Jesus gives his goodness to all who believe. All have sinned and fall short of God's standards, but he freely accepts them by his grace and through Jesus' rescue.
God shows his goodness by offering Jesus as a sacrifice of atonement to pay for their sins.

5.1–11   **Peace and friendship with God**
Jesus gives his people peace with God. They believe and God saves by his grace. They now boast in Jesus Christ.
Rarely will anyone die for someone else, but Jesus died for sinners. His blood saves them from God's anger and restores friendship with God.

Deal given by: ....*Jesus*..................

Deal received by: ....

"Grace"

This is undeserved generosity. People stood as God's enemies, but Jesus pays for their sins and gives them his goodness. His people now stand with a perfect record.

★ ★ ★ ★ ★

How does Jesus save people?

Paul explains some blessings

Paul also explains what a Christian inherits. They receive blessings from their Father in heaven and Paul knows they will make God's people joyful!

KINGDOM MEMBERS
Inheritance List

God the Father chose us to enjoy these blessings before the world began. Members inherit all these blessings:

 ### Holy and Blameless
He gives us goodness, and we have Jesus' perfect record. No guilt!

 ### Adoption
He adopts us as sons and daughters. We are part of God's family!

 ### Life With God
Jesus buys us back with his blood, so we can live with God again.

 ### Forgiveness
He forgives us for all sins: past, present, and future.

God gives us the Holy Spirit to guarantee these blessings. We know we have the Spirit, so we know we have these blessings.

"Inheritance"
No believer can lose their inheritance. They are members of God's family and will live with God again in the new creation. Jesus paid for the inheritance with his life.

★ ★ ★ ★ ★

Why is a Christian's inheritance certain?

Geography: the good news spreads

Paul travels around the Mediterranean three times: over 10,000 miles! He ends his life in Rome, where he awaits trial before Caesar. Paul makes the most of it: he writes letters and even tells his guards about Jesus!

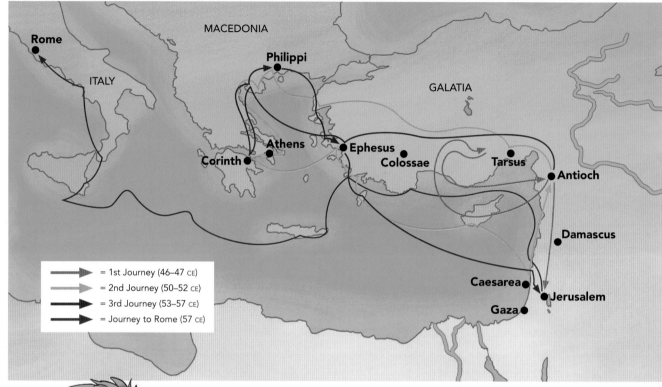

= 1st Journey (46–47 CE)
= 2nd Journey (50–52 CE)
= 3rd Journey (53–57 CE)
= Journey to Rome (57 CE)

ASK 3D FREDDIE

Why was Paul so successful?

He was a well-educated, hardworking, Jewish, Greek-speaking Roman citizen! He became "all things to all men". He became like his audiences to teach them about Jesus.

- **Jerusalem** is where the Holy Spirit first comes and Saul helps kill Stephen.
- **Caesarea** is where Peter meets the Roman centurion Cornelius.
- **Gaza** is where the Ethiopian is journeying to when he meets Philip.
- **Damascus** is where Ananias meets and heals Saul.
- **Antioch** is the starting point for all three of Paul's teaching journeys.
- **Tarsus** is Paul's hometown, where he is raised as a strict Pharisee.

- **Athens** is the capital city of Greece.
- **Corinth** is where Paul starts a group of believers (a church).
- **Ephesus** is where Paul starts a group of believers (a church).
- **Philippi** is where Lydia, the slave girl, and the jailer first believe.
- **Rome** is where Paul appeals to Caesar (the emperor) with a legal case.

Timeline: Jesus and his followers

A lot happens after Jesus is born! In fact, Jesus changes the world. Within just 50 years, Christianity spreads across the Roman Empire and beyond.

Jesus is born.

Jesus, aged 12, teaches in the Temple.

Jesus works in Nazareth as a carpenter.

Jesus begins work as a teacher.

4/5/6 BC   **AD 8**   **8 - 28/30**   **28/30**

Saul becomes a Christian on the way to Damascus.

Saul watches Stephen get stoned to death.

The Holy Spirit comes at Pentecost.

Jesus dies on a cross.

33/34   **31/34**   **30/33**

Peter meets Cornelius in Caesarea.

James (John's brother) is martyred (Acts 12).

Peter is rescued from prison (Acts 12).

Paul's 1st journey.

Peter and Paul meet in Jerusalem (Acts 15).

38   **44**   **46/47**   **48/49**

Paul arrested in Jerusalem (Acts 21).

Emperor Nero rules after Claudius dies, Jews return to Rome.

Paul's 3rd journey.

Emperor Claudius expels Jews from Rome.

Paul's 2nd journey (visiting Philippi).

57   **54 - 68**   **52 - 57**   **49**   **48/49 - 51**

Paul imprisoned in Caesarea by the Romans (Acts 23–26).

Paul taken to Rome by the Romans (Acts 27–28).

Paul imprisoned in a house of the emperor Nero.

Paul released, travels and writes letters, rearrested.

Paul martyred in Rome under Nero.

57 - 59   **60**   **60 - 62**   **62 - 67**   **64 - 67**

ACT 8: NEW CREATION

SCENE 1: NATION HUMANKIND

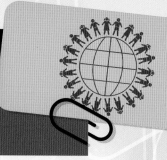

Promises fulfilled

Jesus gives John a Revelation. It's the premiere of his new creation where he keeps his age-old promises to Abraham and David. Countless people are there.

INTERVIEW SPECIAL!
3D FREDDIE MEETS JOHN

3D Freddie: John! You're here to end the Bible story! What should we look at?

John: Look at how God fulfils his promises. Look at God's completed world. Look how Jesus defeats the devil once and for all. Look, and you won't stop looking.

3DF: Wow. Thanks… Where do we carry on?!… So… who was in your vision?

J: I saw a massive gathering from every country, tribe, people, and language. They stood before the throne of God and the Lamb, wearing pure white clothes and carrying palm branches, singing, "Our God saves. Our God and the Lamb."

3DF: The Lamb? An animal sat on the throne?

J: The Lamb is Jesus. Like a sacrifice, he took the punishment his people deserved and now he sits in glory beside God the Father. The people wave palm branches as a symbol of victory. The Lamb has won the fight. Angels sang around the throne, "Praise, glory, wisdom, thanks, power, and might go to God for ever and ever!"

3DF: Wow again! And how will God keep his promises?

J: God promised Abraham he would bless all nations on earth through one of his descendants. All nations on earth will enjoy God's blessing. Also God promised David he would give him a descendant to rule his people for ever and ever. Wonderfully, Jesus fulfils both of these: Jesus, the Lamb and King.

<<< FLASHBACK

… to Passover (page 42). Israel sacrificed lambs, waiting for God to sacrifice the perfect Lamb.

"Massive gathering"

The new nation sees how God keeps his promises. They come from all over the world, and Jesus rules them for eternity. They love to praise their king.

★ ★ ★ ★ ★

How does God fulfil his promises?

The New Heaven and Earth

John sees all of heaven. It's a new creation where God lives with his nation humankind. It's a fully perfect city with fully happy people. And it's fully God's.

·········· PRESS RELEASE ··········

Jesus Christ revealed the future to me. Anyone who hears and believes it is blessed!

I saw a new heaven and earth. The first heaven and earth had gone, the sea too. I saw a new city, a new Jerusalem, coming from God. A voice said from the throne,

"Look and see! God now lives with humankind.
They will be his people and he will be their God.
He will wipe the tears from their eyes,
And death, grieving, crying, and pain will be over.
I am the Alpha and Omega, the A to Z, the start and the end.
The thirsty may drink freely from the spring of the water of life.
I will be their God and they will be my children.
Others, cowards, will live in the lake of fire."

The city measures about 1,400 miles (2,253 km) long, 1,400 miles (2,253 km) wide, and 1,400 miles (2,253 km) high. Its walls are jasper, and inside is gold, clear as glass. The rarest jewels cover the city.

There is no Temple. No need. The Lord God Almighty and the Lamb are the Temple. Humans meet God for real. There is also no sun or moon. No need. God's glory lights the city, beaming from the Lamb. The gates never shut. No need. It is never night and the city is safe. No one unclean will ever enter, only people who have their names in the Lamb's book of life.

ASK POPCORN SALLY

Who goes to the new creation?

Anyone! But not everyone. Often people try to go there by being good or going to church, but the only way is to trust Jesus for forgiveness.

"No one unclean"

Only forgiven people can live with God. They drink the water of life, truly satisfied. The new city is God's home, a perfect cube like the Most Holy Place in the Temple.

★ ★ ★ ★ ★

What is special about the city?

SCENE 2: GOD'S NEW EDEN

God's people reign forever

The new creation is like the Garden of Eden, but better. God brings back what made Eden so good, but this time they will eat from the tree of life and live forever.

The river of the water of life, clear as crystal, running from God's throne through the middle of the city.

The tree of life with twelve crops of fruit, one per month. Its leaves heal the nations.

God and the Lamb Jesus on the throne in the city. He no longer curses anything.

The massive gathering reign as kings for ever and ever.

"For ever and ever"

The new Eden is better than the old. The tree of life gives eternal life and heals the nations. People reign with God as kings for ever and ever, and never stop serving him.

★ ★ ★ ★ ★

<<< FLASHBACK

… to Eden (page 14). There was a river and a tree of life. God walked in the Garden with man and woman, and they looked after it.

How is the new Eden better?

God's last promise

Jesus will return. He said he was leaving to prepare rooms in his Father's house. He said, "I promise, I am coming soon!" The eternal morning is about to dawn.

COMING SOON!

THE LORD GOD ALMIGHTY   THE LAMB   THE MASSIVE GATHERING

THE BRIGHT MORNING STAR

The man who is God returns.

Promised, Produced, and Directed by David's ancestor and descendant.

★ ★ ★ ★ ★

Eden Echo
"Unmissable. But when is the release date?"

★ ★ ★ ★ ★

Future Times
"So worth the wait! This will be talked about forever."

ASK 3D FREDDIE

What's the difference between the two Edens?

Nothing. And everything! The new Eden will be like the first, but so much better! And it lasts for eternity, which never ends. So this is not the end! Later on, folks!

"The bright morning star"

The morning star signals dawn. Jesus will return on a set day to judge the world and begin God's new Eden. No one knows when, but he promises he will. Soon.

★ ★ ★ ★ ★

Why are God's people now waiting?

CAST LIST

Here are 75 names from the Bible story! Can you remember their stories?

Aaron
brother of Moses; first high priest; builds golden calf

Abel
son of Adam and Eve; murdered by his brother Cain

Abraham
father of God's people; almost sacrifices his son Isaac

Adam
first human alongside Eve; sins against God in Eden

Ahab
7th king of Israel; leads Israel to worship Baal

angels
God's servants and messengers; guard way to Eden

Bathsheba
wife of David; David is unfaithful to his wife with her

Boaz
redeemer; "buys back" Ruth by marrying her

Cain
son of Adam and Eve; murders his brother Abel

Caleb
one of 12 spies; tells Israel to trust God for victory

Daniel
prophet in Babylon; is thrown into den of lions

David
2nd king of Israel; receives promise of an eternal kingdom

Deborah
judge who defeats the Canaanites; advises Barak

Delilah
Philistine wife of Samson; cuts Samson's hair

Ehud
judge who defeats the Moabites; stabs Eglon

Elijah
prophet to Israel; calls God to fire up an altar

Esau
elder brother of Jacob; gives up his birthright

Esther
Jewish queen of Persia; rescues Jews in Xerxes' empire

Eve
first human alongside Adam; sins against God in Eden

Ezekiel
prophet to Judah; sees a vision of dry bones

Ezra
expert in God's Law; teaches returning exiles

Father
person of the Trinity of God; Father of Jesus

Gabriel
angel; tells Mary she is pregnant with God's Son

Gideon
judge who defeats the Midianites; fights with 300 men

God
I AM, Yahweh, Lord, Jehovah

gods
many gods; are worshipped instead of God

Goliath
warrior of Philistines; giant whom David defeats

Hebrews
name for the Israelites while in Egypt

Herod the Great
ruler of Judea; directs the wise men to Jesus

Hezekiah
king of Judah; prays for God's rescue

I AM
God's personal name; Yahweh in modern language

Isaac
son of Abraham; prays for sons and gets twins

Isaiah
prophet to Judah;
predicts the Messiah

Jacob
father of 12 sons
and tribes; renamed
"Israel" by God

James
One of 12 disciples;
brother of John;
martyred in 44 BC

Jeremiah
prophet to
Jerusalem; warns
Judah about
destruction

Jeroboam
1st king of the
northern kingdom;
makes idols for Israel

Jesus
Son of God and
Messiah; Jesus
means "the Lord
saves"

John
one of 12 disciples;
writes a book about
Jesus' life

John the Baptist
cousin of Jesus;
baptizes Jesus in the
Jordan

Jonah
prophet to Nineveh;
is carried in a big
fish's stomach

Joseph
11th son of Jacob;
rules Egypt under
Pharaoh

Joseph
acts as father of
Jesus; descends
from David

Joshua
one of 12 spies;
leads Israel after
Moses dies

Judas Iscariot
One of 12 disciples;
betrays Jesus to the
chief priests

Laban
uncle of Jacob; tricks
and mistreats him

Lazarus
raised to life by
Jesus; brother of
Mary and Martha

LORD/Lord
translation of I AM
or Yahweh; God's
personal name

Mary
mother of Jesus;
gives birth as a virgin

Moses
leader–prophet;
leads Israel to the
Promised Land

Naomi
mother-in-law to
Ruth; goes home to
Bethlehem

Nebuchadnezzar
king of Babylon;
sends Daniel's
friends to fiery
furnace

Nehemiah
leader for returning
exiles; rebuilds
Jerusalem's walls

Noah
descendant of
Adam; builds an ark
before the flood

Paul (Saul)
preacher across
Mediterranean;
meets Jesus in a
vision

Peter
one of 12 disciples;
declares Jesus as
Messiah

Pharaoh
king of Egypt;
refuses to release
Hebrew slaves

Pharisees
teachers of God's
Law; criticize Jesus
for loving sinners

Philip
preacher to the
Ethiopian; not one of
12 disciples

Pontius Pilate
Roman governor
in Judea AD 26–36;
crucifies Jesus

Rachel
2nd wife of Jacob;
gives birth to Joseph

Rebekah
wife of Isaac; helps
Jacob to trick Isaac

Rehoboam
1st king of the
southern kingdom;
harshly taxes Judah

Ruth
Moabite widow;
stays with Naomi
and marries Boaz

Samson
judge who fights
the Philistines; tears
down a temple

Samuel
prophet; anoints Saul
and David as king

Sarah
wife of Abraham;
laughs at the idea of
a son

Satan
the devil; means
"the accuser"; is
defeated by Jesus

Saul
1st king of Israel;
makes excuses about
his sin

snake
the devil in Eden;
lies to Adam and Eve

Solomon
3rd king of Israel;
builds the Temple
and turns from God

**Spirit (or Holy
Spirit)**
person of the Trinity
of God; lives in
Jesus' followers

Stephen
follower of Jesus; is
stoned to death

Thomas
one of 12 disciples;
doubts the
resurrection

Xerxes
king of Persia; rules
vast kingdom with
Esther as queen

GLOSSARY

And I bring you 50 pieces of Bible jargon. They're clever words.

ark of the covenant
gold-covered box holding Ten Commandments

ascension
Jesus returns to heaven to sit by God the Father

baptism
water symbolizing washing away sins

blessing
special happiness with and from God

covenant
long-lasting agreement between God and his people

Day of Atonement
when high priest makes sacrifices for Israel's sins

demons
evil spirits who belong to the devil

disciples
followers of Jesus

Eden
place of "delight" where God puts the first humans

eternity
time that never ends in the new creation

exiles
people taken away from their homeland

exodus
mass exit from Egypt

the Fall
when Adam and Eve first sin against God

faith
actively trusting and relying on God

Genesis
creation or beginning

Gentiles
non-Jews; included by Jesus as God's people

glory
praise; or the cloud of God's presence in the Temple

God's kingdom
when people treat Jesus as king

Gospel
book about Jesus' life

gospel
good news about Jesus' death and resurrection

Israel
nation God rescues and treasures

Israelites
God's people; the suffix "-ites" means "people of"

Judgment Day
when Jesus returns to judge everyone with justice

judges
early leaders of Israel against foreign enemies

Law
rules for God's rescued people

manna
honey bread given in the desert

Messiah (or Christ)
Chosen or Anointed One (Hebrew and Greek names)

miracle
act of God breaking the laws of science

Most Holy Place
cube-shaped room in the Temple where God lives

nation
people group with their own land

new creation
new world where God lives with his people

parable
story with a deeper lesson for Jesus' followers

Passover
day when God saves the firstborn sons in Egypt

Patriarch
founding ancestral father of Israel

Pentecost
day when the Holy Spirit comes to live in all believers

priests
worshippers set apart for special work

prophets (prophecy)
messengers or mouthpieces of God

resurrection
day when Jesus rises from the dead

Revelation
book of "revealed things" about the new creation

sabbath
day of rest for God's people

sacrifice
giving up for a greater cause; or offering God something

sin
rebelling and turning away from God's rule

snake crusher
man to defeat sin and death, promised in Eden

Son of Abraham
descendant of Abraham, who blesses the whole world

Son of David
descendant of David, who rules his kingdom forever

tabernacle
portable "tent of meeting" where God lives

Temple
building in Jerusalem where God lives

Ten Commandments
ten laws summing up the 613 laws

testament
agreement between God and his people

transfiguration
when Jesus' clothes turn shining white

CREDITS

This project has been quite an adventure. I wanted to write a Bible overview for children, but the book grew beyond anything I imagined at first. It began as a school book with activities, but this final cut fits on a bookshelf at home, school or church. There are countless people I want to thank for their ideas and support over the last nine years. Here are a few. • Heather Henderson planted the idea as she encouraged me there was space in the market and that self-publishing was always an option. That was Christmas 2010! • Thanks go to Vaughan Roberts for the eight-Act structure in his excellent Bible overview *God's Big Picture* which helped inspire this book. • Peter Alessi helped write synopses as I approached publishers, and Rob Perry taught me graphic design for months before I wrote the trial book. • Lots of friends helped to proofread, test, discuss, and develop the ideas here and in *The Teacher's Cut*. Particular thanks go to Jonny Burgess, Jack Charnley, Susan Grenfell, Larry and Sinead Norman, Harry Paget, Anthony Rendall, and Phil Steen. It's been a long time coming! Thanks also to the countless others who closely followed the project and helped to refine its ideas. • Thanks go to my pupils for showing me what they liked reading and also for how enthusiastically they spotted typos! • Big thanks go to David Horrocks and Matt Searles for proofreading the book's theology and expression. Thank you, David, for years of faithful Bible teaching, and to Matt for the "Living with God" theme in this book. • Suzanne Wilson-Higgins opened the door at Lion Hudson at a time when I may have self-published. Deborah Lock, Jacqui Crawford, Luca Cretan, and Margaret Milton have been consummate professionals in how they took this from script to shelf, and Collaborate have designed and illustrated it with understanding and good humour. Thank you. • I also owe a debt to Eric Prydz whose music has been the soundtrack to much of my writing. • Most of all I want to thank my parents. My father, Peter, taught me that if something is worth doing then it's worth doing well, and my mother, Clare, was the first to point me to Jesus. This book is for them.